Set Boundaries and Restore Yourself

A Woman's Practical Guide for How To SAY NO to Excessive Demands by Family, Friends, and Work. Finally Get the Time You Need

George Munson

GL DIGITAL PUBLISHING LLC

Contents

Introduction

You're tired. Not just the kind of tired that more sleep can fix. This is the deep exhaustion that comes from giving too much, too often. Maybe you always show up for family, friends, partners, and work. You're the one people count on, always keeping the peace. Still, you might wonder: When will it be your turn to rest? When will someone ask what you need? If you've ever felt stretched thin or invisible in your closest relationships, you're not alone. This book is for you.

Setting boundaries isn't about shutting people out. It's about choosing yourself, with the confidence that you deserve respect and care. Many of us learned that putting our needs first is selfish or rude. We worry about hurting others, being judged, or losing love and connection. But boundaries aren't barriers. They're a way to show self-respect. They help you show up as yourself and care for others without losing who you are. Boundaries aren't just for protection; they're acts of self-acceptance and courage.

This book comes from years of listening. I've worked with many who feel guilt or fear when they try to say "no" and have seen how cultural norms and expectations shape our ability to speak up. My goal is to help you build boundaries that honor your life, values, and relationships. Honoring your needs is a commitment to your well-being.

We need practical solutions that work in real life. Many books talk about boundaries, but few offer clear steps for the tough situations you face daily. Even fewer recognize that boundaries aren't "one size fits all." What works for one person or in one culture might not fit your world. You deserve guidance that respects who you are and where you come from. This means being honest about your unique challenges, whether with family traditions, workplace power dynamics, or friendships that leave you drained.

If you've tried to set boundaries before, you might have faced resistance. Maybe someone called you "difficult" or "selfish." Maybe you felt guilty for putting yourself first or worried about what would happen next. Maybe you wondered if healthy boundaries were even possible for you. I see these struggles. I know it can feel risky to change old habits. In these pages, you'll find scripts for tough conversations, strategies to handle pushback, and tools to manage the emotions that come with change. Remember, growth takes time, and setbacks are part of the process. Be gentle with yourself as you learn.

This book isn't about blame or quick fixes. You won't find shaming language or unrealistic promises. I won't tell you to cut off everyone who challenges your boundaries or pretend all relationships can be fixed. Instead, you'll get real guidance for overwhelming family requests, friends who lean too much on you, and authority figures who pressure you. You'll learn to navigate differences and care for yourself even when others don't understand.

You will discover a clear, step-by-step process for creating boundaries that fit your circumstances. By following these steps, you'll learn how to identify your needs, set limits confidently, and maintain healthier, more supportive relationships.

- Real-life scripts for saying "no" with clarity and kindness

- Strategies for handling guilt, fear, and anxiety

- Blueprints for boundaries in love, work, and family

- Ways to manage resistance and consequences

- Tools for ongoing maintenance and repair

- Practices to build confidence and compassion for yourself

You won't find empty platitudes or judgment here. No advice ignores your reality. I respect that you know your life best. My role is to walk beside you, offering guidance, support, and encouragement as you move forward.

I wrote this book because every woman deserves to feel safe, respected, and heard in her relationships. I'm passionate about helping women move from survival mode to confidence and calm. Change is possible, and you are worthy of it. Boundaries aren't a wall, they are doorways to deeper connection, better health, and a life that feels like your own. You have the strength to create that life.

As you read, you might feel both hope and fear. That's normal. Setting boundaries asks us to step into discomfort, but also into our own power. I invite you to be gentle with yourself. Celebrate small wins, and keep going even when it feels hard. Remember, change is a process, and each step forward is progress. You're not alone in this work. Every page is written with understanding, respect, and the belief that you are worthy of care.

Let's begin this journey together. Let's move from exhaustion to empowerment, from silence to self-expression. The path won't always be easy. It will be worth it. Your needs matter. Your voice matters. You matter.

It's time to choose yourself.

Chapter One

Why Boundaries Matter Now

It's 10:30 PM. Your phone lights up: your sister asks for a babysitter, your boss sends an "urgent" email, and a friend needs breakup advice. After a long day of work and errands, you feel pressured to say yes to everyone. Even feeling grateful doesn't stop the exhaustion that comes from giving when you have nothing left to give. If this sounds familiar, it's not a sign of weakness. It's what happens when you don't have boundaries.

The Boundary Burnout Epidemic Is, In Part, Why Women Are So Exhausted

Let's call it what it is: a burnout epidemic. It may not make the news, but it slowly wears down your energy and spirit. Burnout often starts small, saying yes to extra work, helping a friend, or hosting family at the last minute. Over time, these moments accumulate into a heavy emotional load. Studies show that women often bear the burden of invisible work, such as tracking details, smoothing over arguments, and being the "default" helper for partners, friends, and family. This mental load is constant, mostly unnoticed, and rarely returned.

It's more than just picking up the slack; there's a deeper cost. You might lie awake, worrying if you upset someone or regretting saying yes instead of no. Maybe you keep track of everyone's moods, always trying to keep the peace. Being the go-to supporter can feel noble, but it can also make you feel invisible. The requests persist, your phone goes off during dinner, weekends, or when you need quiet. It can feel like your time and energy never truly belong to you.

Always being emotionally available leads to "boundary burnout." It causes stress and drains your life. Your sleep suffers, your body feels it, and patience and joy fade into irritability and resentment. Over time, your desires get lost under everyone else's needs.

Women are often called the strong one, the reliable one, or the fixer. At work, this means taking on extra projects because "you always get it done." At home, you remember every family detail, even if no one notices. Among friends, you're the one expected to drop everything for any crisis. The unspoken expectation: you'll handle it all, no matter your exhaustion.

But we rarely talk about the cost. When your boundaries are weak, you lose more than just free time; your mind can't relax, so you lose real rest. Resentment builds in relationships. Your self-worth takes a hit as you start to measure it by how much you give. Many women admit they feel like they're failing at everything, even when doing most of the work.

It's more than just working harder or organizing more; it's about empowering yourself to set clear boundaries. Permit yourself to say "Enough," and intentionally carve out time for your well-being. Start small, choose one area where you feel most depleted, and set a boundary there. Your exhaustion is a signal that you can take control and make a change, and you have the power to start right now.

Before we move forward, take a moment to check in with yourself.

This reflection will help you recognize where burnout most affects you, validating your experience and encouraging self-understanding. Take five minutes to write down where you feel most drained, in your body, your mood, or your thoughts. Is it at home, with friends, or at work? Noticing this is the first important step.

You deserve to rest, and now is the time to claim it. Take one action this week, such as saying no where you usually say yes, or asking for help instead of handling everything alone. It's normal to feel guilty or worried about conflict, but remember, setting boundaries is a form of self-respect. Treat boundary burnout as a red flag calling you to choose yourself. You have the right to protect your time and energy, and every step you take is progress toward something better. Trust that your boundaries will improve your well-being and relationships over time.

Identify How Toxic People Hijack Your Energy By Spotting the Invisible Drain

Some people are just hard to get along with. Others leave you feeling exhausted, even after a short conversation. A truly toxic person leaves a pattern: repeated guilt trips, manipulation, or ignoring your needs. For example, some friends always reach out only in times of crisis, coworkers who give you their work at the last minute and insist you can't say no, or relatives who use guilt to get their way. The word "toxic" is often used, but here it means someone whose behavior consistently drains your energy, confidence, or peace of mind. You might also hear "energy vampire," someone who frequently feeds on your emotions, leaving you feeling emptier each time. These aren't just people having a bad day. Over time, such patterns can make you question your reality, your worth, and sometimes even your sanity. Recognizing these subtle signs helps you catch boundary issues before they escalate.

What makes a truly draining person different? It's the pattern: bit by bit, they take more than they give. The signs aren't always clear at first. A guilt-tripper might sigh, "After all I've done for you, this is how you repay me?" A gaslighter might say, "You're just too sensitive; I never said that," making you doubt your reality. Some friends never ask about your life; instead, they regularly call only to unload their own crises. Boundary-pushers might be coworkers who give you last-minute work, or siblings who expect you to adjust your plans immediately for them.

It's Friday night, and you're looking forward to a quiet evening, but your phone rings. It's a friend you care about, but she only calls when something is wrong. Tonight, she's in tears again over the same relationship drama. You spend an hour, then two, listening and offering comfort, while your own plans fall by the wayside. When the call ends, you feel drained and even a bit resentful. You wonder if you're being selfish for feeling this way. Now, think about Monday morning. Your coworker asks for help "just this once" to finish a project. You already have too much to do, but she insists she has no one else to help. You stay late, skip lunch, and miss your workout again. Or maybe it's family. Your mother uses guilt, saying things like, "If you really loved me, you'd come over right now." Each of these situations chips away at your energy and makes you doubt yourself.

Toxic people rely on others' emotional labor. They rarely respect boundaries and focus on their own needs. Sometimes this is manipulation; other times, it's just learned behavior. The result is real exhaustion and self-doubt. Time with these people leaves you drained, even physically, and sometimes questioning your reality.

Are You Dealing with an Energy Vampire?

- Do you regularly feel anxious or obligated before seeing or speaking to someone?

- After interactions, do you feel emotionally wrung out or resentful?

- Does this person dismiss your feelings or twist events to make you doubt yourself?

- Are their needs always urgent, but yours go ignored?

- Do you find yourself rearranging your plans to accommodate them, often at your own expense?

- Is guilt or fear of conflict the main reason you stay connected?

If you answered "yes" to several of these, you're not imagining the impact these situations have on your well-being. Subtle manipulation can be harder to notice than obvious abuse, but the result is the same: your energy is taken for someone else's benefit.

Awareness is the first step to taking back control. You have the right to name what's happening. Your feelings are valid. Don't stop at noticing these invisible drains; take action to address them. Recognize the patterns, understand that your exhaustion has a real cause, and commit to making changes that restore your energy.

People-Pleasing Isn't Your Fault; Unpacking Social and Cultural Traps

From an early age, many girls are praised for being "good," helpful, agreeable, and eager to keep the peace. Whether from family, teachers, or the approving smiles of strangers when you sacrifice or assist, society quietly instructs girls to be nurturing and accommodating. As you grow, these expectations intensify. The world applauds the peacemaker, the one who never says no, who quietly mends conflicts and rarely seeks anything in return. Pop culture reinforces this message: heroines win admiration when they put others first without asking for anything in return. We see countless examples in movies and TV where a character's value seems tied to how much she's willing to give up for others.

Family dynamics add another layer. Especially as the eldest daughter, you might feel heightened pressure to be responsible and emotionally available. Maybe you're called on first for chores, to mediate fights, or tend to a parent's needs. Sometimes the expectation is clearly stated: "Set an example for your siblings." Other times it's more subtle, like the unspoken relief when you quietly fix problems no one else addresses. Over time, you internalize these expectations until they become automatic scripts. Your role is to keep everyone around you happy, even at your own expense.

These beliefs run deep. People-pleasing becomes automatic: you say yes when you want to say no, force a smile when you're upset, or apologize for things you didn't do. You start to link love and acceptance with being accommodating, and soon, letting others down feels scarier than losing yourself. Social media makes this worse, always praising women who "do it all" with a smile, while rarely discussing boundaries or self-care.

Popular shows like "This Is Us" and "Gilmore Girls" show this pattern. The daughters rush to meet everyone's needs while ignoring their own pain. Even when they're overwhelmed, viewers are encouraged to admire their selflessness instead of asking why they always have to sacrifice. Romantic comedies praise women who put others first and often label those who set boundaries as cold or difficult.

It's important to know that people-pleasing isn't a flaw or weakness. It's something you learn, shaped by family roles, culture, and society's ideas about how women should act. It's not hardwired; it's copying what you see rewarded and what gets criticized.

If you've been called a "nice girl" or "good daughter," remember these are roles given to you, not your true worth. Underneath these learned behaviors is someone with her own opinions, needs, and boundaries, someone who deserves care and respect just as much as anyone else.

Here's the most empowering truth: if you learned to people-please, you can also unlearn it. You're not stuck. With awareness and effort, you can change these patterns and respond differently when others expect you to put yourself last.

You Learned This, And Now You Can Learn Something New

- Pleasing others developed as a survival skill.

- Saying yes became a habit.

- Guilt was handed to you, not innate.

- Boundaries can be built, step by step.

- Self-worth grows each time you honestly express yourself.

Understanding this helps free you from shame or self-blame. The urge to please comes from deep social conditioning, not from a personal failing. With awareness, you can choose which old patterns to keep and which ones to change for yourself.

Real-Life Snapshots of What a Healthy Boundary Actually Looks Like

Boundaries can be confusing because you can't see them, but you definitely feel their effects. Imagine boundaries as a fence with a locked gate, not a brick wall. The fence marks where your yard ends and your neighbor's begins. You decide when to let someone in, when to step out, and when to close the gate and take a breath. A healthy boundary protects your space without cutting you off from others. There's still a connection, but it's mutual, respectful, and on your terms.

Let's look at three approaches: having no boundary, a healthy boundary, and a wall. With no boundary, you say yes even when you want to say no. You answer texts at midnight, take on extra shifts you can't handle, or let friends vent for hours without a break. You end up feeling resentful, unseen, and maybe even lost. A wall is the opposite; it's rigid. You block people out, refuse to share your feelings, or avoid any request, even reasonable ones. It might feel safe at first, but it soon feels lonely and cold. A healthy boundary is in the middle. You might say, "I can't make it tonight, but I'd love to catch up this weekend," making room for both your needs and the relationship.

Here's how this looks at work. A manager comes by your desk with another urgent task. Instead of saying yes right away, you reply, "I'm at capacity with my other deadlines. Can we decide which project is most important?" This isn't defiance, it's being clear. You're not saying "never," just "not everything at once." It's honest, respects your limits, and stays professional.

In friendships, boundaries show up when you say no to an invitation without feeling guilty or needing to explain. Your friend asks you to help her move again, but you're exhausted from the week. A healthy response could be, "I'm not able to help with moving this time, I hope it all goes smoothly!" You show you care, but you don't apologize for having your own needs. Compare this to forcing yourself to go and feeling resentful, or ignoring her call; both extremes can hurt trust and create distance.

In relationships, boundaries let you be close without losing yourself. Maybe after a long day, you need some quiet time instead of doing things together. You tell your partner, "I need an hour alone to recharge, let's hang out after." You're not pushing them away; you're letting them know what helps you be your best self later. This brings honesty to the relationship instead of silent frustration.

Setting boundaries with family can be the hardest because traditions and expectations run deep. Imagine a relative who expects you to visit every Sunday, but is also the only time you have to rest. Instead of avoiding calls or always giving in, you gently explain, "I can't visit every Sunday anymore, but I'd love to plan for once a month." This isn't rejection, it's caring for yourself and for the relationship in the long run.

Healthy boundaries aren't ultimatums or punishments. They let others know what you need to feel safe, respected, and energized in any relationship. When set well, boundaries actually make relationships stronger by allowing for honesty. Everyone knows where they stand and what's possible together. You don't have to be perfect or strict; boundaries are flexible and can change over time.

A boundary isn't about control. It's about mutual respect, yours and theirs. When you set a boundary, you're saying, "My needs matter too." This encourages others to do the same, building relationships based on trust instead of silent sacrifice or hidden resentment. Boundaries keep relationships healthy; they let you be yourself without fear of being ignored or overwhelmed. Like a garden fence, they protect what's important while still letting in sunshine and conversation.

Busting the Myths of Why Saying "No" Isn't Selfish or Mean

It's hard to shake the feeling that saying "no" makes you the bad guy. Maybe you've heard it from others, or maybe your inner critic says, "If I set boundaries, people will leave. I'll be alone." Or, "Turning someone down means I don't care about them." These fears stick because we hear them everywhere, at home, in movies, or from friends who don't understand what healthy boundaries are. But here's the truth: saying "no" doesn't make you cold or uncaring. It just means you're human, with your own limits and needs. Think about the oxygen masks on a plane; flight attendants always tell you to put on your own mask first. You're not ignoring others; you're making sure you can help if you're able. That's what boundaries do. They help you keep giving without running on empty.

The idea that boundaries push people away is common, but reality is different. Research and real-life stories show that when women set boundaries, they often gain more respect and healthier relationships. People who truly care about you want you to feel safe, seen, and valued, not always drained. Boundaries make room for honesty; they don't build walls, but open doors for real connection. Sometimes, the people who get upset or try to guilt you when you set a limit are the ones who benefit from your lack of boundaries. That discomfort isn't a sign you're wrong; it's proof you're finally putting yourself first. While a few people might pull away, the relationships that matter will get stronger and more real.

Another common worry is that saying no means you don't care. Actually, it's the opposite. When you say yes out of guilt or obligation rather than real desire, resentment and exhaustion start to build. Over time, you might avoid calls or dread spending time together. Real care can't last if you're always running on empty. Healthy boundaries let you show up fully, honestly, and willingly, because you've protected your own energy first. It's the difference between giving someone your full attention and just going through the motions.

The voice of the outer critic can be loud: "You're being difficult." "You used to be so nice." But often, "nice" means "easy to ignore" or "easy to manipulate." What if we thought of "nice" as being clear? What if kindness meant telling the truth about what we can and can't give? To quiet both inner and outer critics, try a few new ways of thinking. "No is a complete sentence." You don't owe anyone a long excuse. "Self-care isn't selfish," it's self-respect. If someone pushes back when you set a boundary, remind yourself: "I am not responsible for other people's reactions to my limits." Each time you use one of these reminders, notice how it feels, maybe anxious at first, but then replaced by relief and pride.

Boundaries aren't about rejection or punishment; they're invitations to be honest in your relationships. When you say no to things that overwhelm or hurt you, you're also saying yes to your health, your peace, and your most important relationships. You make space for joy, creativity, and rest. Imagine what could grow in your life if you let yourself choose where your energy goes.

Every time you choose your well-being over automatic people-pleasing, you start building deeper connections with others and with yourself. Saying no isn't just about protecting yourself; it's a powerful act of self-love that makes every yes more meaningful and every relationship more real. This isn't selfishness; it's wisdom and courage in action.

Chapter Two

Getting Clear, Personal Boundary Self-Assessment

The "Boundary Barometer" Quiz to Pinpoint Your Personal Patterns

Many women move quickly, trying to please or avoid conflict, and miss these patterns. To build real boundaries, slow down and honestly see where you're strong and where you struggle. This awareness fosters confidence and a sense of control over your choices. Think of this quiz as a way to spot your patterns, like finding potholes on a map.

The "Boundary Barometer" quiz helps you see your habits more clearly. It's a guide, not a test. You'll review situations such as a mom visiting unexpectedly, a friend needing help late at night, a boss giving extra work, or a partner wanting attention when you need alone time. For each, choose your honest response, even if you wish it were different. There's no right or wrong, just be truthful.

The Boundary Barometer Quiz

1. Your mom texts that she'll visit in an hour, but you planned a quiet night.
   - ○ A) Tell her tonight doesn't work; suggest another time.
   - ○ B) Feel awkward but agree.
   - ○ C) Ignore her and hope she doesn't come.
   - ○ D) Offer a brief visit as a compromise.

2. A colleague needs you to cover her shift, but you're exhausted from plans.
   - ○ A) Decline politely.
   - ○ B) Say yes and feel guilty.
   - ○ C) Ignore the request.
   - ○ D) Propose swapping shifts.

3. Your partner wants to discuss something heavy late at night when you're drained.
   - ○ A) Say you'll talk tomorrow when rested.
   - ○ B) Listen anyway, even if tired.
   - ○ C) Pretend to be otherwise occupied.
   - ○ D) Suggest a short talk now, the rest later.

4. A friend wants to go out after a long week, but you'd rather recharge.
   - ○ A) Thank her but decline to stay in.
   - ○ B) Say yes and regret it.
   - ○ C) Make an excuse at the last minute.
   - ○ D) Suggest a quiet alternative or another day.

5. Your sibling asks for a loan, but you're saving for something.
   - ○ A) Explain your situation and say no.
   - ○ B) Lend the money and feel stressed.
   - ○ C) Avoid the conversation.
   - ○ D) Offer other help, not financial.

Now, when you've finished going through each situation, total how many times you selected A, B, C, and D. Compare your totals to the descriptions below to better understand your approach to boundaries:

- Mostly A's: Strong boundaries - you're clear and direct, prioritizing your needs.

- Mostly B's: Over-Extender - you default to yes, often at your own expense.

- Mostly C's: Avoider - you dodge tough conversations, but often feel uncomfortable or resentful.

- Mostly D's: Negotiator - you seek compromise, but sometimes bend further than you'd like.

If your answers are a mix, that's completely normal. Most people find some situations easier than others. Recognizing these differences can spark curiosity about your blind spots and motivate growth. Seeing these diffcrences helps you spot both your strengths and areas for development, fostering a mindset of ongoing self-discovery.

Here's what your profile says

Over-Extenders are valued for kindness but risk neglecting their own needs; learning to say no is self-care, not rejection. Avoiders dislike conflict and often learned to keep the peace by being silent, but this can lead to resentment. Enforcers (A's) are steady and consistent, though they may appear rigid. Negotiators balance everyone, sometimes at their own expense.

Remember, your boundary profile is a starting point. Save your answers and revisit them in a few months to track your progress. Noticing changes in your responses can boost your confidence and help you refine your boundary-setting skills over time, reinforcing that boundary development is an ongoing journey.

Quiz Summary

Take a moment to record your "Boundary Barometer" profile and your insights:

- My dominant pattern(s):

- One area I do well:

- One area for improvement:

- Something I learned:

- Date:

Put this summary somewhere you'll see it often, like your mirror, fridge, or planner. It's a reminder that boundaries aren't set in stone; they get stronger the more you practice.

Use Values Mapping to Define What Truly Matters to YOU

Many of us react automatically, not knowing why some requests drain us or why certain boundaries are hard to keep. Instead of focusing only on saying no, ask: What am I protecting? Your values hold the answer. They guide choices, shape relationships, and clarify why things feel right or wrong. Knowing your values can inspire a sense of purpose and make boundary setting feel more authentic and aligned with who you are.

Starting with values means choosing what matters to you rather than meeting others' expectations. Take a piece of paper or your notes app and do a "values brainstorm." Write any words that feel important, don't judge or edit yourself. Your list might include freedom, creativity, rest, honesty, loyalty, growth, peace, adventure, connection, stability, fun, or faith. Maybe you value laughing with friends, quiet time to recharge, or speaking your truth. It's normal for your values to shift over time.

After you have your list (try for at least ten words), look it over and circle the ones that feel most true to you. Don't worry if your choices differ from anyone else's; this is about what matters to you, not what looks good to others. If "rest" stands out, it might mean you need to protect your downtime. If "honesty" is most important, you'll probably feel uncomfortable when you can't speak openly or are expected to pretend. For some, "family" means joining Sunday dinners; for others, it means keeping distance from family drama. Only you know what brings you real peace.

It's common to have unclear boundaries when your values aren't clear. That's when you might overcommit, say yes when you want to say no, or feel resentful without knowing why. When your values are blurry, your boundaries are too, and you may end up following someone else's rules while feeling lost. But when you know what matters, it's easier to set limits. If "rest" is important but your weekends are packed, you'll notice burnout sooner and feel more confident saying, "I need this Saturday for myself." If you value "creativity" but your days are full of draining tasks, it's time to make space for creative work.

To put this into action, use the format below. Write your "Top Values" on the left side and take a moment to think about them. Then, narrow your list down and circle the top five, go with your instincts, and remember you can always change them later. Next to each value, write one way a boundary could help protect it in your daily life.

For example:

- **Rest Boundary**: No work emails after 7 p.m.

- **Honesty Boundary**: Speak up when I disagree, even if my voice shakes

- **Connection Boundary**: Prioritize regular one-on-one time with my partner

- **Creativity Boundary**: Block out Sunday mornings for art, no social plans

- **Stability Boundary**: Say no to last-minute requests that mess with my routine

Then, fill in this sentence:

"My boundaries protect my value of _________."

There's no right answer; whatever rings true for you.

Treat this as a living document. Come back to it whenever life changes, or you notice yourself falling back into old habits.

Spend a little time thinking about how ignoring your values in the past has led to feelings like resentment, exhaustion, or regret. Remember times when you said yes but felt uneasy afterward, or when someone kept crossing your boundaries and left you feeling small. Try journaling with this prompt: "Describe a time you felt resentful after saying yes. What value was compromised?" Maybe you gave up rest for someone else's urgent request, or kept quiet instead of being honest. Write freely, without holding back.

Now, think about a time when you felt totally comfortable in a relationship or social situation. Maybe a friend respected your need for quiet nights, or a boss supported your work-life balance. Try this prompt: "When did you feel most at peace in a relationship? What value was honored?" Notice how much better you felt when your core needs were respected.

The clearer you are about your values, the less likely you'll be to feel guilty or pressured by others. Your boundaries become less like walls and more like invitations for people to get to know the real you, the person who knows what she stands for and protects it with confidence.

Identifying Your Top 5 Boundary Blind Spots

Think back to the last time you left a conversation feeling tense or kept replaying it in your mind. Maybe you agreed to something you didn't want to do, or set a limit but didn't stick to it. Blind spots with boundaries do more than cause small mistakes; they quietly shape your choices, drain your energy, and leave you feeling powerless. Most people have a few, often in the areas that matter most to them. You might not notice these blind spots until you're overwhelmed or exhausted for the third week in a row. Once you spot them, you can start to see the patterns that keep you stuck.

One common blind spot is overcommitting, saying yes to everything, like school bake sales, early airport rides for friends, or hosting holiday dinners even when you're busy. It might seem generous, but it's often driven by guilt or fear of letting people down. You might tell yourself, "It's just this one time," but soon your schedule is packed with things that don't help you. The exhaustion builds slowly. For example, if your neighbor asks you to watch her dog for the weekend and you agree even though you need rest, you might feel cranky and resentful by Sunday, upset that you didn't honor your own needs.

Another blind spot is unclear communication. You might think you're setting a limit, but your words sound unsure, like "I'm not sure if I can..." or "Maybe I could help, but..." These phrases slip in because you don't want to seem rude. But your real message gets lost, and others may take your uncertainty as a yes. For example, if your boss gives you extra work and you say, "I guess I can fit that in," even though you're already overwhelmed, she hears yes, and your workload keeps growing while your needs are ignored.

Rescuing is another blind spot, jumping in to fix other people's problems without being asked. It can make you feel helpful, but it often leaves you drained. For example, if a friend calls upset after a fight with her partner, you might rush to offer solutions before she's even finished talking. Later, she feels better, but you're left carrying her stress and ignoring your own needs.

Fear of conflict can also weaken your boundaries. If someone sounds annoyed or raises their voice, you might back down or change your mind to avoid an argument. You might think it's not worth the fight, so you let things go to keep the peace. For example, if your partner brings up a tough topic, you might stay quiet instead of sharing your thoughts to avoid a disagreement. Over time, this can lead to resentment, not only toward the other person but also toward yourself for not speaking up.

Another blind spot is not following through. You might set a boundary, but then not stick to it. For example, you tell your family that Sunday mornings are for sleeping in and not for calls, but when someone calls early, you answer anyway. Each time you give in, it gets harder to keep your boundaries, and others start to see your limits as optional.

Here's a quick self-inventory to help you spot common blind spots:

- I often agree to things I don't actually want to do.

- I say yes reflexively without considering my needs.

- I use unclear language like "maybe" or "I'll try" instead of being direct.

- I rush to solve others' problems without being asked.

- I change my mind if someone reacts negatively

- I set boundaries but rarely stick to them.

- I feel resentful after conversations where I didn't express myself.

Check off the statements that feel true for you; these are probably your main blind spots.

Mini-scenarios clarify blind spots in action: Overcommitting is saying yes to a party when you need rest; not following through is reminding your partner about chores, then doing them yourself; fear of conflict is lending money to a friend again without raising the issue of repayment to avoid awkwardness.

To change these habits, try keeping a log of blind spot reflections. After any situation where you feel uncomfortable about your boundaries, write down: What was the blind spot? What happened? How did you react? What could you try next time, maybe clearer words, pausing before you answer, or asking for time to think? Over time, these reflections can help you respond differently.

Be kind to yourself as you become aware of your blind spots. They come from old habits and beliefs about what's safe or acceptable. Try to see them without judgment and treat each one as an opportunity to try something new. Small steps, like pausing before saying yes or giving one clear answer, help you get better at setting boundaries. Writing down your experiences shows your progress, and over time, you'll notice old patterns more easily and appreciate how you're protecting your energy and peace.

Recognize Your Triggers, Learn When and Why You Struggle to Speak Up

Some situations affect you more than others. Maybe it's the way your dad's tone changes when he asks for help, or how your partner's silence feels heavy after you say you need space. Sometimes it's just an email from your boss asking you to help out, even when you're already overwhelmed. These aren't just random stresses; they're emotional or situational triggers. Certain people, topics, or settings can make it really hard to hold your boundaries or speak up. You might not even notice your body tensing or your heart racing until it's over and you're left wondering, "Why did I freeze up again?"

Triggers often come from past experiences, like old landmines. Maybe when you were a kid, saying no meant getting punished or ignored, so now the idea of disappointing someone makes you anxious. For many women, conflict feels more than just uncomfortable; it can feel unsafe, because rejection has become linked to love or safety. If your family saw disagreement as disrespect, standing up for yourself now might bring up strong feelings of guilt or anxiety. At work, if a manager's disappointment once cost you a promotion, even a small criticism can make you feel small, even if you know your boundaries are important.

When you map out your triggers, they become less confusing, and you have a better chance of responding rather than just reacting. Think about the last few times you had trouble setting a boundary or felt uneasy after talking with someone. Who was involved? What did they ask? How did your body and mind react? Maybe your mom asked for a favor on a weekend you wanted to rest, and you felt tense but said yes anyway. Or your partner raised his voice during a disagreement, and you stayed quiet to avoid conflict. Maybe your boss sent a late-night request, and you felt anxious, so you replied right away without checking your schedule.

To get clearer, use a simple "Trigger Tracker" list. Fill it in for three situations that stand out from the past two weeks. For example:

Who/When
  What's asked.
  How I feel,
  How I react.

Mom/Saturday
  Watch her dog last minute.
  Guilty, tense,
  Say yes, cancel plans.
Boss/Tuesday PM
  Finish extra report overnight.
  Anxious, pressured,
  Agree quickly.
Partner/Evening
  Talk after work when exhausted.

Irritated, trapped,
Listen anyway.

This chart isn't meant to make you feel bad; it's about helping you become more aware. You'll start to notice patterns, like certain people always making you feel guilty, or certain topics bringing up fear. Sometimes your reactions are automatic, shaped by years of trying to avoid conflict or rejection. These patterns often come from earlier experiences. If you grew up around yelling or silent treatment, it makes sense that raised voices now make you want to hide. Or if love always meant giving up your needs, it's still hard to say no to loved ones

Knowing your triggers is a big step, but learning to pause before you react can make all the difference. When you notice that old feeling, maybe your breath quickens or your mind races; permit yourself to take a moment. You don't have to answer right away or fix everything immediately. Try saying, "I'm feeling overwhelmed, let me check my schedule and get back to you tomorrow," or "I want to think about this, can I answer in the morning?" Taking this pause interrupts the automatic yes and gives you space to decide what you really want and need

It might feel hard at first, but the old urge to please or avoid conflict will come up. But each time you practice pausing, even for a few seconds, you start to change those old habits. Over time, your body learns that setting boundaries isn't dangerous. It can become a normal part of your conversations.

Triggers don't usually go away completely, but they lose their power as you start to notice them and respond on purpose instead of automatically. The more you practice tracking your triggers and pausing before you react, the more confident you'll feel when tough moments come up.

As this chapter ends, remember that awareness is the first step toward change. By looking at your patterns, getting clear on what matters, spotting your blind spots, and understanding your triggers, you're already making progress toward real self-respect. In the next chapter, we'll talk about using clear language and practical scripts to express your boundaries, so you'll have tools ready even when you feel nervous or unsure.

Chapter Three

Scripts & Communication Techniques for The Language of Boundaries

Breaking Down the Script of a Boundary Statement

Setting a boundary can shift the atmosphere in a room. If you have ever wondered whether you could have said something differently, you are not alone. Many women have not been taught to express their needs clearly and kindly. The most important part is having a structure: know your intention, speak, and keep your tone steady. This is a skill you can learn. With practice, it becomes easier and more natural. Remember, each boundary you set is a step toward feeling more in control and confident in your relationships.

Start your boundary statement with clarity about what you want to communicate, so you can articulate boundaries confidently and handle pushback effectively. Know what you want, then say it directly. Keep your request short; brief statements are less likely to be misunderstood. Show empathy by acknowledging the other person's feelings, but don't ignore your own needs. Speak with confidence and don't apologize for your request. One helpful way to do this is: "When you [behavior], I feel [emotion]. I need [boundary/request]." This keeps the focus on your experience instead of making assumptions about the other person.

For Example:

- "When meetings run late without notice, I feel anxious because of childcare responsibilities. I need us to stick to the agenda, or let me know about changes."

- "I can't take on this extra project, but I can help brainstorm solutions."

Each statement is clear and specific, without blaming anyone. You share your point of view and say what you need, which helps prevent misunderstandings.

Speaking assertively can help you feel calmer. Using direct language lets you express yourself instead of holding things in until you get upset (see Source 1 in the APA list). Being assertive isn't about being harsh; it's about respecting both yourself and the other person. Your tone should be steady and not apologetic. Use "I" statements instead of blaming. Good posture and eye contact also help get your message across, much more than crossing your arms or looking away. Remember, it's okay to stand firm and handle pushback with calm confidence, which reassures you and others that your needs matter.

People often confuse assertiveness with aggression or passivity, but these are separate. Assertiveness means clearly sharing your needs while respecting others, as in statements like "I'm not available for that" or "I need more notice." Aggression, by contrast, ignores others' needs and can come across as blaming or critical, such as "You never think about my time!" Passivity puts others' needs above your own, as in "It's fine, I'll just do it," and does not express your needs. So, assertiveness balances self-respect and respect for others, aggression prioritizes your needs over others', and passivity prioritizes others' needs over your own.

Templates can make it feel less daunting to speak up. Try:

- "When you ____, I feel ____. I need ____."

- "I can't ____, but I can ____."

- "I'm not able to ____ right now."

- "I care about our relationship, so I need to ____."

Use these templates to set boundaries and prepare for potential pushback, helping you respond confidently and maintain your limits. For a softer boundary, you could say, "I appreciate the invite, but I can't this time." For a firmer statement: "I'm not available for that, and I need you to respect my decision." If someone needs reassurance, try: "I care about you, but I need to take care of myself right now." Each template respects both you and the other person. Next, let's explore how to use these techniques when you need to say no, particularly with family, friends, or coworkers.

Write Your Own Boundary Statements

Practice writing and saying your boundary statements to build confidence and reduce guilt when you need to say no. Think of a recent time when you didn't speak up. Using the templates above, write three versions of your statement: one gentle, one firm, and one empathetic. Notice how the tone changes with each. Practice saying them out loud or write them down before your next conversation. The more you practice, the easier it gets, and you'll feel more ready to use these words when you need them.

"No" Without Guilt, Scripts for Turning Down Family, Friends, and Colleagues

Saying "no" can sometimes feel challenging because of others' expectations. When a family member calls, you may worry about letting them down. At work, your boss may offer another project, and you might hesitate in refusing. Friends might ask for favors when you are tired, and you could fear seeming selfish. For many women, saying no brings guilt and concern about disappointing others. This worry can lead to overcommitment and resentment. Remember, you have the right to set limits, even if others don't like it. Your boundaries are a form of self-care, and saying no is a way to protect your well-being and feel more secure in your choices.

Remember, you have the right to set limits, even if others don't like it. Guilt often comes from caring, but you can acknowledge their feelings without ignoring your own. For example, if a family member wants your help every Sunday, you can say, "I know it's important for us to spend time together, but I need this weekend for myself." This is honest about your needs, not a rejection. With practice, using direct but caring scripts gets easier. At work, if you're overloaded, try, "My schedule is full right now, so I can't take on more." If a friend wants to talk but you're tired, say, "I can't talk tonight, but let's catch up soon. I want to be present for you when I have more energy."

These scripts avoid too much explanation or apologizing. Wanting to justify every boundary often stems from a desire to be "nice," but saying more can lead to negotiation and doubt. Short responses like "I don't have the bandwidth right now," or "I can't help this weekend, but I hope it goes well!" are both clear and kind. If you want to soften your answer, suggest another option that works for you, like "I can't make dinner tonight, but maybe coffee next week?" or "I'm not available for extra hours, but I can help prioritize."

Even with these strategies, it is common to feel guilty or anxious, concerned about letting others down. This is normal, especially if you have learned to prioritize others' needs. Yet saying yes when you mean no does not support genuine relationships; over time, it can erode trust and happiness. Instead of making excuses, allow yourself a pause after you speak. A brief silence gives your words more impact and shows that you are confident in your decision.

Your body language helps reinforce your boundary. Stand relaxed but upright, make eye contact, and keep your tone calm. Avoid apologizing or speaking too softly. If declining face-to-face feels difficult, practicing your words out loud or writing them down first can help you stay steady.

Handling Pushback

If someone keeps asking after you've said no, don't get pulled into an argument. Repeat your answer: "I've already said I can't this time." If family tries to make you feel guilty, remember that their upset doesn't mean you're wrong; it just means they're getting used to your boundaries.

Learning to say no without guilt takes time. You might make mistakes or slip into old habits. But each time you use these scripts and speak with confidence, it gets easier. You'll change how others see you and how you see yourself. Your needs are important, too.

Saying Yes to Yourself, Or, How to Request What You Need (and Get It)

Asking for what you need can feel powerful, especially if you were taught your needs were too much. Saying yes to yourself isn't selfish; it helps you take care of yourself. Start by letting go of the idea that your needs matter less than others'. If you need time alone, say it: "I need some downtime tonight to recharge." If you want help, ask: "Can you take care of dinner this week?" These words are simple but can feel hard to say at first. It's normal to worry about sounding demanding. That anxiety means you're learning new habits.

When you ask for what you need, you might hear a voice in your head saying, "You're being difficult," or "Don't rock the boat." Try to replace those thoughts with reminders like "My needs are valid" or "Self-care helps everyone." These help you stay steady when guilt comes up. Taking care of your own needs actually lets you be more generous and present with others. You're not pulling away; you're making sure you have the energy to show up for people in a real way.

Sometimes people push back when you ask for change. Your partner might look disappointed when you ask for space, or a friend might tease, "You've gotten so picky lately." When this happens, it's important to negotiate, but remember your limits. Instead of giving in or getting defensive, try saying, "I can't do X, but I could help with Y." For example, if your roommate wants to talk every night and it's too much, you could say, "I'm not up for talking tonight, but I can chat with you tomorrow morning." This way, you offer a solution while still taking care of yourself.

Role-playing can really help. Practicing your boundary statements in front of a mirror can calm your nerves before a real conversation. Say your request out loud, like, "I need Saturday to myself, I've had a draining week." Watch your expression. If you notice yourself shrinking or fidgeting, try to stand tall. Repeat your words until they feel more comfortable. If speaking out loud feels too hard at first, write your thoughts in a journal. Write out different situations that have been tough for you. For example: "Hey Mom, I know we usually talk every night, but I need some quiet evenings this week." Practicing ahead of time makes the real conversation feel less scary and more natural.

It can help to write down a few scripts before situations like big family gatherings or work meetings, so you're ready if things get emotional. If holidays wear you out, you might say, "I'll be leaving by 7 tonight so I can rest." If you're overloaded at work, try, "I'll need help prioritizing if more tasks get added to my list." Planning for pushback helps you keep your boundaries clear and fair.

Remember, saying yes to yourself doesn't mean others will always be happy or understand right away. That's their process, not a reason for you to give in. Over time, people will start to respect the boundaries you set. Each time you use clear words, whether you're asking for time alone or for help, you show that your needs matter too. The more you practice, the more natural it will feel to speak up for yourself.

Handling Pushback in the Moment For Real-Time Rebuttals to Manipulation and Guilt-Tripping

Boundaries aren't always easy for others to accept. Sometimes, when you set a clear limit, people push back with guilt, sarcasm, or even anger. Some may try to pressure you into changing your mind. When this happens, it helps to have words ready to protect your boundary. You don't have to explain yourself over and over. Just stay steady, firm, kind, and keep it brief.

If someone tries to make you feel guilty when you say no, like if your mom says, "You're being selfish," you might feel ashamed. But you can calmly answer, "Taking care of myself helps me show up better for others." If a friend says, "You never have time for me," reply, "This is about today, not every time. I can't make it right now." If someone raises their voice or complains, you can say, "I hear that you're upset, but my decision stands." You don't have to manage every feeling that comes up when you set a limit.

Dealing with anger or tension can be hard, but staying calm is your best tool. If things get heated, say, "Let's take a break and talk later." This helps cool things down and shows you won't get pulled into drama. If someone keeps pushing, you can say, "I'll revisit this if things change, but I need you to respect my answer." You don't have to give an immediate or detailed explanation. Sometimes, repeat yourself: "I'm not changing my mind." Or, "This isn't up for debate."

It's easy to want to explain yourself, hoping others will understand your side. Try not to. Long explanations often lead to more arguments and weaken your boundary. Trust that a simple "no" or a clear statement is enough. If you feel like you need to keep talking, pause and take a breath. Remind yourself it's okay to stop at one sentence: "No explanation needed." Sometimes, silence is your best tool.

Passive-aggressive reactions are another challenge. This might look like sarcasm, such as "Guess I just don't matter," or the silent treatment. Don't get pulled into defending yourself or apologizing for your needs. You can say, "I notice you're upset, but my boundary hasn't changed," or, "I understand this is hard for you." Recognize their feelings, but don't change your limit.

Pushback and Responses

Manipulative Response: Assertive Boundary Statement" You're being selfish. "Taking care of myself helps me show up better for others. "You never help anymore. "This is about today, not the past. "But you always do it for me! "Today I'm choosing something different for myself. "Raised voice/anger: "I hear you're upset, but my decision stands. "Passive-aggressive silence or sarcasm: "I notice you're upset; my answer hasn't changed. "Repeated requests after a 'no', "I've answered already, I'm not available." Emotional escalation: "Let's pause and talk when we're both calmer."

When you get pushback, whether it's guilt-tripping or subtle manipulation, your main job is to stay steady. You don't have to fix their feelings or take on their frustration. Say your decision once, maybe twice, then leave it at that. Even if you feel nervous, each time you do this, you show yourself and others that your boundaries matter. Over time, people will see that pushback doesn't change your mind; it only makes you stronger.

Text, DM, or In Person? Adapting Boundaries for Digital Communication

These days, boundaries aren't just tested in person; they come up online too, in group chats, DMs, work messages, or late-night emails from your boss. The digital world can make things easier, since you can think about your words and even keep a record of what you said. But it also has downsides. Without tone or body language, your words might seem blunt or cold, even if you mean well. Emojis can help, but only to a point.

It's important to know when to use digital boundaries and when to talk in person. If a conversation might be emotional or needs empathy, like telling a friend you can't support them as much as they need, it's usually better to talk face-to-face or on the phone. You can hear their tone and see their reactions. For routine things, like scheduling or reminders, text or email works well. For example, if you need to turn down an invite or set work limits after hours, a quick message can save time and reduce stress.

When you use scripts online, keep them short, clear, and direct. You want to sound friendly, not robotic, and avoid long back-and-forths. For a text, you might say, "Hey! I can't make it tonight, but thanks for thinking of me." In an email: "I'm not available for extra hours this week." These are friendly and clear, and don't invite more negotiation. In DMs, you can be even briefer: "Not free tonight, hope you have fun!" If you're worried about sounding cold, add a smiley or a quick note like "Hope we can catch up soon."

Pushback online can be tricky. Sometimes people guilt-trip you in group chats, like saying, "But we always do this together!" Or someone keeps messaging after you've already said no. It might seem easier to ignore them, but being clear is kinder and more effective than disappearing. You can say, "I've already answered this, and my answer hasn't changed." If a group chat gets dramatic or passive-aggressive, you can mute it or leave with a simple message: "Taking a break from this chat for now, see you all soon!" You don't have to give a detailed explanation for your digital boundaries.

Managing your availability is just as important as what you say. Use your phone's "Do Not Disturb" in the evenings so you're not tempted to reply right away. Muting notifications after work tells others, and yourself, that your downtime is off-limits. If people expect quick replies, let them know: "I'm offline after 7 pm and will reply in the morning." For work emails, you can set an auto-reply: "Thanks for reaching out, I'll respond during business hours." For friends, pre-written responses like "Can't talk right now; will check in tomorrow" save energy and help keep your boundaries clear.

Digital boundaries protect your peace as much as your time. Just because it's easy to send messages doesn't mean people should have access to you all the time. Allow yourself to be unavailable sometimes—not every group chat needs your reply, and not every DM needs an instant answer. How you set boundaries online affects how people treat you in other areas, too.

To wrap up, remember that every boundary, online or in person, is about making your needs seen and respected. Your words matter, wherever you use them. Next, we'll look at how to use these skills at home and with family, where things can be more complex, but also where real change can begin.

Chapter Four

Boundaries at Home for Navigating Family Dynamics

Taming the "Drop-In" Dilemma, Stopping Unannounced Visits (Without Family Drama)

After a long day, surprise visits can feel overwhelming, especially if you're not ready for company or want some time alone. It's normal and healthy to want privacy when unexpected guests show up.

It can be tough to set boundaries if your home has always felt like a shared family space. You might feel guilty about changing things or worry that your family will think you're being selfish. Still, your home is your own, and it's perfectly reasonable to ask for notice before visits.

Share your needs clearly and calmly, such as, "I appreciate our time together, but notice helps me prepare." Focus on expressing your needs without criticizing others' actions.

If face-to-face talks are hard, try a polite sign requesting visitors call or text ahead, or send a group message before busy times: "I need some downtime this weekend; let's plan if you'd like to drop by." Setting expectations this way helps everyone.

Family may resist limits, expressing disappointment or mentioning past habits. Respond with empathy: "I know this is a change; notice helps me." Offer alternatives: "Let's pick a regular day." This keeps the connection while respecting boundaries.

In some cultures, having an open-door policy is a long-standing tradition, so setting boundaries can feel especially hard. It can help to frame boundaries as small adjustments: "Family is welcome in our culture, and I value that. Sometimes I need rest. Can we balance both?" Bringing your family into the conversation shows you respect both tradition and your own needs.

Setting boundaries can be tricky when generational differences are present. Older relatives might not be accustomed to privacy and may see new rules as unnecessary. Stay consistent in your response: "It helps me be a better host if I know you're coming." With time, most families get used to these changes.

Your "Visit Values" Inventory

Spend a few minutes journaling about what matters most to you for family visits at home:

- When do you feel most comfortable having visitors?

- How much notice helps you prepare?

- What emotions surface with unannounced drop-ins?

- What did you learn about family and privacy growing up?

Write one sentence about what would make family visits joyful, not stressful. Use this as your guiding statement in difficult conversations.

You deserve a peaceful, safe home where you can recharge. Setting boundaries isn't rejection; it helps everyone's needs get met and avoids misunderstandings. Asking for notice is healthy.

When Siblings Cross the Line for Money, Favors, and Emotional Blackmail

Sibling relationships can be complicated. There's a special closeness, but also a unique tension. If you're seen as the 'responsible one,' your boundaries with your siblings might blur. Maybe you're the first person they call for babysitting, rides, or advice. Sometimes it's about money. small loans or splitting costs unfairly. Other times, it's favors like helping with moves, watching pets, or running errands because 'you're so good at this.' It can hurt when you say 'not this time' and notice the mood shift. You might hear, 'But family always helps family,' or get the silent treatment for days.

Emotional blackmail can show up in sibling relationships. It might look like guilt trips. 'If you really cared, you'd help.' Sometimes it's silence after you set a boundary, or passive-aggressive comments like, 'I guess I can't count on anyone.' There may even be threats: 'Don't forget who was there for you last year.' These tactics can leave you feeling trapped or doubting your boundaries. It's not always easy to spot, since people often dismiss these behaviors as 'just how we are.' But ongoing guilt and manipulation are warning signs, not harmless quirks.

It helps to get clear about what's really going on before you respond. If your sibling asks for something and you feel dread or obligation instead of wanting to help, take a moment to pause. Ask yourself: Is this a one-time thing, or just the latest in a long list of requests? Do I feel comfortable saying no, or does it make me anxious? Paying attention to these feelings can help you spot manipulation before you get caught up in it.

Am I Being Emotionally Manipulated? A Quick Checklist

- Do you feel guilty every time you say no to your sibling?

- Is silence or withdrawal used as punishment when you set limits?

- Are there threats (even veiled ones) about what will happen if you don't help?

- Does your sibling bring up past favors as leverage?

- Do you feel responsible for fixing their problems more than your own?

If you answered yes to several questions, emotional blackmail is probably happening. The main points: notice when you feel ongoing guilt or pressure. These are warning signs. Trust your discomfort as a sign that it's time to set stronger boundaries.

Once you notice the pattern, stick to your boundaries with simple language: "I'm not able to lend money right now," or "I can't watch the kids this weekend." If requests continue, renegotiate: "I can help once a month, not every week." Consistency helps siblings adjust over time.

If your sibling gets angry or tries to guilt you by saying things like, "We're supposed to stick together!" acknowledge their feelings, but don't give in. Stay calm and say, "I care about our relationship, and I hope we can respect each other's limits." If things get tense, they might stop calling or complain to other family members about how "cold" you've become. Give it some time and space to cool off. You don't have to chase after them or fix their mood. Sometimes, letting things settle for a few days helps everyone calm down without saying things they'll regret.

It can feel awkward to reconnect after a conflict, but it's often healing if you come from a place of care and steadiness. When things have cooled down, reach out with something neutral, like, "Hope things are going well. I want us to move forward." Try not to bring up old arguments. Focus on what's ahead. If your sibling wants to talk about it again, stay firm but kind: "My boundaries aren't about not loving you; they help me show up honestly." Sometimes, siblings need to hear that love and support don't mean you're always available.

If you still feel resentful or stuck in old habits, take a step back and write down what feels fair to you. Journaling can help you see which requests are reasonable and which ones leave you feeling drained. If you can, talk openly about sharing responsibilities, splitting costs with other siblings, or making a schedule for favors so no one gets overwhelmed.

Boundary-setting with siblings is rarely comfortable, but honoring your needs builds healthier relationships. Consistency shows that your limits are commitments and leads to less resentment. Key takeaways: Keep limits clear, communicate steadily, and remember boundaries foster healthier bonds.

Eldercare and Parental Guilt, Setting Limits with Aging Parents

Caring for aging parents can feel like an emotional marathon. You might find yourself torn between love, responsibility, family expectations, guilt, and exhaustion. If you're part of the "sandwich generation," balancing the needs of kids, work, and parents, the pressure can be overwhelming. Even if you want to help your parents, constant demands can leave you feeling drained, resentful, and unsure of your own needs.

It's common to feel like you owe your parents endless support, especially because of cultural values or family expectations. Many people feel caretaking is expected, especially if you're the eldest daughter or the sibling who "has it together." Memories and family stories can make this sense of duty even stronger. It's hard when your mom says she's lonely or your dad talks about the past, and guilt can take over as you watch them age.

But your needs are important too, even if other people's needs seem more urgent.

No one can do it all; there are limits to what you can handle physically, emotionally, and financially. Respecting these boundaries isn't abandoning your parents; it's being honest. Ask yourself what you can realistically offer without burning out. Maybe you can do grocery runs every other week, but daily visits are too much. Perhaps you can handle medical appointments if someone else handles paperwork or phone calls. Being honest about what you can do helps prevent resentment and keeps you from making promises you can't keep.

Once you know what's realistic, share your boundaries with kindness and honesty. This might be tough, especially if your parents aren't used to hearing "no" from you. Be clear but gentle: "I love you and want to help, but I can only do groceries every other week. I can't do daily check-ins because I need time for my family and myself." If your parent feels hurt or guilty and says, "After all I've done for you…," stay steady. Recognize their feelings, but also stand by your own: "I know this is hard, and I'm grateful for everything you've done. I'm doing what I can, but I need to take care of myself, too." Feeling some guilt is normal, it doesn't mean your boundaries are wrong.

If you're being asked to do more than you can handle, share the responsibility; it's not a failure, it's necessary. Talk with your siblings about dividing up tasks and be specific: "I can handle Monday appointments, but I need someone else on weekends." If family help isn't possible, consider outside support such as home health aides, meal services, or community programs. Sometimes, getting extra help is the only way to make things work for everyone.

Dealing with guilt or emotional appeals from parents takes patience and practice. If your parent says, "I never thought I'd be alone so much," or, "You'd understand if you were in my shoes," respond with empathy but stick to your boundary: "I wish I could be here more, but this is what I can manage right now." If they compare you to others, avoid getting drawn in:

"I know everyone's situation is different. This is what works for my family and me."

Cultural expectations can make these talks harder, especially when duty or respect for elders is important. In these cases, using respectful language helps. Acknowledge your family's values: "Mom, I know we've always helped each other in our family." Then gently share your boundary: "With my work and the kids, I can visit every Sunday, but not during the week." Using honorifics or formal words can soften your message: "Papa, I respect everything you've given us; I want to help, while caring for my own health too." Remind them that boundaries protect everyone: "If I burn out, I won't be able to help anyone."

Making a written schedule or care calendar can keep expectations clear and show your ongoing commitment without having to renegotiate constantly. For example: "Grocery runs, second and fourth Saturdays; phone check-ins, Wednesdays." Having things in writing helps parents and siblings adjust to new routines.

Remember, protecting yourself from exhaustion isn't selfish; it lets you be truly present with your parents. Clear boundaries mean you're less likely to burn out and more able to respond with patience and warmth. While guilt is a normal part of this process, remind yourself that loving someone also means caring. If things get emotional, pause before you respond. Even saying, "I need some time to think about how I can help," gives everyone a chance to cool down. Setting boundaries with aging parents isn't always easy or welcome, but it's a way to respect both them and yourself. Over time, it helps everyone adjust to new realities with more understanding, kindness, and grace.

Cultural "Shoulds" vs. Personal Needs, Respecting Roots While Creating Your Own Rules

Family often shapes how we act, sometimes before we even notice it. Maybe you remember your mom telling you to "be a good girl," or your grandmother saying that eldest daughters should sacrifice for everyone else. There might be an unspoken rule that keeping the peace means never speaking up. These expectations, whether said out loud or not, can make it hard to know what you really need. You might notice this when you hesitate to speak up at family gatherings or feel guilty for skipping a tradition to rest. Every culture has its own "shoulds," passed down like family recipes. While these can give us a sense of belonging, they can also make it hard to put our own needs first if we never question them.

It can be confusing when what you want doesn't match what you were taught to value. Maybe you grew up thinking daughters should always put family first, or that "good children" never question their elders. You might say yes to things that cross your limits because you're afraid of being seen as selfish. This pressure can be especially strong for women, especially in cultures where respect is tied to obedience. Feeling caught between honoring your roots and taking care of yourself is real and valid. It doesn't mean you love your family less—it just means you're starting to recognize your own needs, too.

Figuring out which cultural "shoulds" no longer work for you takes courage. Pay attention to the voices you hear when you try to set boundaries. Whose words come up? Which sayings stand out, like "Family comes first," "Don't rock the boat," or "We don't say no to elders"? These are clues to beliefs that might not fit your life now. Try journaling about it: "What family rules or sayings do I hear in my head when I set boundaries?" Writing them down can help you see what still fits and what you're ready to let go.

When you notice a family "should" that doesn't fit your needs, try to reframe it instead of rejecting it completely. You don't have to turn your back on your heritage or blame your family to take care of yourself. A balanced way is to show gratitude for your culture while sharing your needs. For example: "I'm grateful for our family's closeness, and I also need downtime," or "I respect our culture, but I need to put my mental health first right now." This way, you honor both your roots and your needs, making it less likely others will feel defensive and more likely they'll listen.

How you talk about boundaries depends on your family's style. If your family values directness, clear statements work best: "I can't come this weekend because I need to rest." If your family prefers a softer approach, gentle language helps: "I wish I could be there; let's find another way for me to connect." Your tone is important, especially if you're the first to set boundaries. Try to keep your delivery warm and steady, showing you're not rejecting them, you're just taking care of yourself.

Compromise can help when family expectations feel strict. If going to every event is too much, try adjusting: "I'd love to come for dinner but need to leave early," or "Can I help set up, then head out before it gets late?" For caregiving, suggest realistic options: "I can help on Saturdays, but I need Sundays for myself," or "Let's divide responsibilities more fairly." Even small changes can ease the pressure and show others what's possible.

Sometimes, showing what you need is about actions, not just words. In some families, being present means love; in others, giving space shows respect. If you're expected to text all day but it wears you out, set a limit: "I'll send a check-in each evening instead of all day." If your family likes to make group decisions but you need time to think, say, "I'll let you know tomorrow." Adapting doesn't mean turning away from your background, it means staying connected in a way that works for you, too.

You'll probably feel some guilt or get pushback; change is always noticed in close families. When someone challenges you, calmly restate your needs or remind yourself of your reasons: saving your energy, protecting your mental health, or enjoying family time without resentment. If others don't agree, remember that taking care of yourself now can encourage others to do the same in the future.

Balancing your own needs with cultural expectations isn't about picking one or the other. It's about blending both to create a life that feels real and sustainable. When you respect your roots and make space for yourself, boundaries can connect generations rather than divide them. As you keep reading, remember: your family roots are important, but so is your right to create your own path.

Next, we'll explore how these patterns show up with friends, and how setting boundaries in those relationships can actually bring you closer.

42

Chapter Five

Friendship Boundaries, Healing the "Therapist Friend" Trap

The 2 AM Crisis Call, How to Say "I Can't Be Your Therapist."

It's after midnight. Your phone lights up, and your friend is calling again in distress. You know, picking up means another hour revisiting the same crisis. You care, but dread these calls; you've become her on-call counselor, regardless of your own needs.

If this sounds familiar, you're not alone. Many women fall into the "therapist friend" role without realizing how much emotional work it takes. We often hear that friendship should be supportive and loyal, but rarely discuss how unbalanced it can get when one person acts as the unofficial mental health hotline. At first, being the go-to friend can feel good, important, and trusted. But when every hangout becomes a therapy session, the emotional drain builds. Soon, you might dread your phone and feel guilty for needing space or rest.

It's important to know the difference between being a supportive friend and acting as an unpaid therapist. In healthy friendships, support goes both ways. If you're always the one helping your friend through emotional crises, especially at the cost of your own rest, it's a sign things are out of balance. You're carrying a weight no one friend should have to, and this isn't just inconvenient. It's about boundaries, your energy, and your mental health.

Noticing this pattern is one thing, but changing it is another, especially if you're used to being the helper. You might worry that setting limits means you're abandoning your friend, but healthy boundaries don't mean you don't care. They show you value your own well-being and friendship. It's possible, and necessary, to be both caring and assertive.

So, how do you say, "I can't do this anymore," without feeling mean? Try gentle honesty. You could say, "I care about you, but I don't have the skills or energy to help with everything you're facing." This sets limits with compassion. If it's late and you need sleep, try, "Can we talk another time? I really need to rest." When topics need professional help, gently suggest, "This might be something a therapist can help you work through." These responses show care while clearly setting boundaries.

You might get some pushback. Your friend may call you insensitive, try to make you feel guilty, or say that "no one else understands." This is tough, especially if you're used to keeping the peace. But it's not your job to fix her feelings about your boundaries. Your job is to stick to what's healthiest for both of you. Calm responses help, such as: "I want to be here for you as a friend, but I need to look after my own well-being," or "Our friendship is important, and I want it to work for both of us." These show you care about both of you.

Changing the conversation takes practice, but it's important. Keep some helpful resources handy, such as crisis lines for emergencies, local therapist contact information, or links to online mental health directories. For example, you can text, "I found this crisis hotline if you need support right now." This way, you show you care while guiding her to help you can't give.

Mental Health Resources and Sample Support Message

- **National Crisis Text Line:** Text "HOME" to 741741 (24/7 support)

- **988 Suicide & Crisis Lifeline:** Call or text 988

- **Therapy Directories:** Psychology Today (psychologytoday.com), Therapy for Black Girls (therapyforblackgirls.com), Inclusive Therapists (inclusivetherapists.com)

- **Sample Message:** "Hey, I care about you, but I'm not able to give this the attention it deserves right now. You might try reaching out to [Crisis Text Line/988] or seeking out a therapist who can help more deeply than I can as a friend."

If guilt persists, remind yourself: boundaries make true friendship sustainable. You're not wrong for needing rest or space. By stepping back from the therapist role, you protect your well-being and the health of the friendship. Honest boundaries build real, lasting connections.

Ghosting, Flaking, and Energy Vampires, Holding Friends Accountable

Friendship sometimes feels like a minefield of expectations, and nowhere is this more obvious than when you're dealing with ghosting, flaking, or that friend who drains every drop of your energy. Ghosting happens when someone you care about suddenly disappears, stops answering texts, won't pick up calls, and leaves you hanging with zero explanation. Flaking, on the other hand, is about repeated last-minute cancellations. Maybe you've put on makeup, gotten dressed, and set aside your evening for a friend, only to get a "Sorry, can't make it!" text ten minutes before meeting. Over time, these patterns make you question your own value in the relationship. Then there's the energy vampire, the friend who always takes but rarely gives. They dominate every conversation with their own drama or needs, but vanish when you could use a little support yourself. Their presence feels less like companionship and more like a matter of survival.

When these behaviors continue, they erode trust. Ghosting makes you feel invisible, flaking makes you question your plans, and energy vampires leave you drained. These patterns lead you to lower your expectations, and soon, resentment grows. It's not petty to notice this; it's honest. You deserve friendships where both people make an effort and value your time.

Being direct can change everything. If a friend keeps canceling or disappears for weeks, it's okay to bring it up. Try saying, "I noticed you've canceled the last few times. Can we talk about what's up?" This opens the door for honesty without blaming anyone. You might find out your friend is struggling or doesn't value the friendship as much. Either way, it's better to know than to wonder. If someone always dominates the conversation or leaves you feeling drained, it's fair to mention it: "I value our friendship, but sometimes our talks leave me feeling really drained." This isn't blaming; it's asking for balance. Or if making plans feels pointless, say: "I want our plans to feel solid. Can we figure out a way that works better for both of us?"

Sometimes, even after you talk about it, nothing changes. That's when you need to protect yourself more. If your friend keeps canceling or disappearing, set a consequence for your own peace: "If this keeps happening, I'll need to step back for a while." This isn't a threat; it's just saying what you need to feel safe in the friendship. If conversations are still one-sided and you feel used or ignored, it's okay to say, "I need friendships that feel more balanced." These statements set clear boundaries without drama.

The hardest part is when nothing gets better, or when your honesty is met with defensiveness or guilt-tripping. Maybe your friend turns it around on you, saying things like, "You're being dramatic," or, "I'm just busy." Or maybe they pull away even more after you bring it up. This hurts, but it also tells you where you stand. You have every right to protect yourself from ongoing disappointment. Sometimes that means changing how the friendship looks, seeing them less often, or moving them from a close friend to a casual acquaintance.

Letting go is tough. We don't talk enough about friend breakups, but they can hurt just as much as romantic ones. If you decide to step away, closure is important. You might say, "I wish you well, but I need to focus on relationships that are mutual." You don't have to give a long explanation unless you want to. You're allowed to choose peace and mutual respect over constant frustration.

It's normal to grieve the end of a friendship, so don't rush yourself. Write down what you'll miss and what you won't. Make a list of happy moments and painful ones. Let yourself feel angry, sad, or even relieved; it's okay to have all those feelings at once. You might talk it out with someone who understands what it's like to lose a friend. Give yourself the same kindness you'd offer after any loss.

Friendships need trust, respect, and real care to grow. When those are missing, it's not selfish to hold others accountable or step back. Setting boundaries is self-respect, not coldness. Make space for mutual, authentic connection and let your friendships thrive.

When Support Becomes a Burden, Setting Limits on Emotional Labor

Friendship can start to feel one-sided before you even notice. It might start with a friend texting whenever she's upset, calling when she's overwhelmed, or using every catch-up to talk about her latest stress. You're always the one listening, nodding, and offering comfort, but you rarely get the same in return. Soon, you realize you're in the "support system" role, and it's not a two-way street. What used to feel mutual now feels like an obligation. If you're always listening but rarely heard, that's a big warning sign. You might notice your stories get interrupted or ignored, or your needs are treated as an afterthought. The pattern is clear: emotional dumping goes one way, and your own struggles stay silent.

If your stomach drops when the phone rings, or you sigh before opening another long message, you're probably carrying more than your share. Maybe you've told yourself, "She needs me," or believe that good friends always listen. But real friendship is about give-and-take, not being someone's permanent emotional sponge. If you feel drained after every call or crave quiet when you see her name, it's time to check in with yourself. Emotional labor isn't just listening; it's taking on someone else's moods, solving their problems, and sometimes giving up your own peace for their comfort.

Changing this pattern starts with honest words. You don't have to be harsh; you can be clear and still care. Try saying, "I love being there for you, but I also need space to share what I'm going through." This puts your experience at the center without blaming. Or say, "Can we take turns listening to each other?" If you want to point out the imbalance, try, "I've noticed I'm doing most of the listening lately. Can we make some time for what's going on with me, too?" These aren't accusations; they're requests for mutual care.

Sometimes you can't take on anyone else's feelings; maybe you're overwhelmed or simply too tired. In those moments, try drawing a gentle line: "I can't be fully present for this right now, let's talk tomorrow." This gives your friend a clear message without shutting her out. If you're also running on empty, say, "I want to support you, but I'm also dealing with a lot myself." This isn't selfish; it's honest and helps prevent resentment from building up.

Sometimes, the best way to reset a friendship is to start new habits. Try making an "emotional check-in" agreement before diving into heavy topics, and ask each other if it's a good time to talk. You could say, "Is this a good time for a vent session?" or "Do you have the energy to listen right now?" This small pause gives both people a chance to say yes or no without guilt. You might also set a time limit for tough conversations: "Let's talk about this for fifteen minutes, then switch topics so we both feel lighter." Setting time limits protects your energy and keeps conversations from getting overwhelming.

If supporting your friend feels like unpaid therapy, it might be time for more structure. A "support swap" calendar can really help. You could take turns each week, with one person sharing first, or set up regular check-ins where everyone gets equal time to talk. Putting these swaps on your calendar keeps everyone accountable and ensures no one is always the listener or the talker.

Sometimes, your friend's needs are more than friendship can handle. If her struggles are ongoing, intense, or triggering for you, encourage her to reach out to a support group or a professional who can help regularly. You can say, "It seems like this is really weighing on you; maybe talking to a group or counselor would help take some of the pressure off both of us." This isn't rejection; it's caring for both her and yourself.

Friendship should make you feel seen and supported, not drained and invisible. When support starts to feel like a burden, it takes courage to ask for balance and honesty to set boundaries around your emotional energy. Every time you speak up about your needs, you foster a healthier connection and remind yourself and your friend that your feelings matter, too.

Signs Your Role Has Become Unsustainable

- You are always the listener but rarely get asked about your own life.

- Conversations feel draining rather than energizing.

- You feel anxious or annoyed when she reaches out.

- You notice resentment building after every call or text.

- Your needs are consistently minimized or dismissed.

- You struggle to share challenges without being redirected back to her issues.

- After hanging up, you feel exhausted instead of comforted.

Use this checklist as a gentle way to check in with yourself. If several points sound familiar, your boundaries need attention. Honoring them will protect both your friendships and your peace of mind.

Making Space for Yourself, Saying No to Plans Without Guilt

It's hard to let friends down. Guilt can show up as a lump in your throat, a pit in your stomach, or hesitation before you reply in the group chat. You want to stay connected, but sometimes you need rest. Maybe you've had a tough week or want some time alone, but the pressure to say yes can feel overwhelming. In active social groups, there's often an unspoken rule that saying no means missing out. Family or cultural norms can make it worse, treating declined invitations as rude or saying that being close means always being available. But needing time alone doesn't mean you care less; it's just human.

Saying no can feel awkward, especially if you start to wonder if your reasons are "good enough." You might feel like you need to make excuses or apologize too much, but you don't owe anyone a long explanation for needing downtime. Simple, direct answers work best and help ease anxiety. For last-minute invites, keep it short: "I'm having a quiet night in, let's catch up soon!" If you know ahead of time you'll need space, try, "I need some solo time this weekend, but I hope you all have fun." Even, "Thanks for inviting me, but I'm not up for it tonight," is enough. These phrases set clear boundaries, reduce guilt, and stop long back-and-forths. You might worry this sounds cold, but real friends usually understand or learn to respect your honesty.

If someone pushes back, be honest about your feelings: "I know I'll miss out, but I need to recharge. See you next time!" This shows you care about the group but also value your own needs. If anyone tries to guilt-trip you, remember their reaction is their responsibility, not yours. You can say, "I hope you understand, this is something I need for myself." Putting your well-being first isn't selfish; it actually helps you be a better friend in the long run. When you take care of yourself, everyone benefits.

FOMO, fear of missing out, is real. Seeing photos of friends having fun without you can sting, even if staying home was the right choice. It's easy to feel left out or worry you're missing new inside jokes. In those moments, remind yourself why you chose to stay in. Write down how good it feels to rest, or what you'll enjoy doing with your free time. Take care of yourself, have some tea, go for a walk, or start that book you've been putting off. FOMO fades faster when you're enjoying your alone time.

Boundaries work best when you set them in advance. Make regular "protected time" for yourself so friends know it's not personal, just part of your routine. Try saying, "I'm making Thursdays my self-care night, let's plan another day." This normalizes rest and helps friends adjust, avoiding drama. Some women even block out recurring calendar slots for downtime, like "Sunday afternoons, me time," and treat them as non-negotiable.

If someone insists or tries to change your mind, like saying, "Come on, just this once!" calmly repeat, "I really need this night for myself." You don't have to explain why rest matters; decide it's important. As you make this a habit, others will adjust, and you'll probably get less pushback over time.

Friendships grow with honesty and mutual respect. Saying no kindly and clearly, without long apologies or complicated excuses, encourages your friends to respect your boundaries and do the same for themselves. This caring approach strengthens your relationships, far beyond just one missed event.

Take a moment and ask yourself: When was the last time you let yourself skip something just because you needed rest? What would change if you put your well-being first more often? These aren't selfish questions. They help you build a life that really fits you.

As this chapter on friendship boundaries ends, remember that a real connection can handle honesty and the occasional "no." Protecting your time isn't just about avoiding burnout; it makes room for joy and realness in every relationship. As you start thinking about boundaries at work, keep this in mind: standing up for your needs isn't rude or distant; it's the foundation for everything meaningful you'll build next.

Chapter Six

Boundaries at Work, From Burnout to Balance

How to Tell Your Boss "No" Without Torpedoing Your Career

Have you ever felt your heart race when your boss sends another 'urgent' project, saying it's 'just this once' or 'shouldn't take long'? You want to help and keep your good reputation, but you're already stretched thin, and your priorities get pushed aside. The challenge is setting boundaries: how do you say 'no' without risking your reputation or future? Many women in their mid-twenties to forties face this, especially if being agreeable feels tied to job security.

Start by reviewing each request before responding. Not every task is urgent or part of your job. Ask: Is this time-sensitive, or is it just a last-minute problem? Does it fit your job description, or is someone else offloading? Be honest about your workload. Can you add this new task without other priorities slipping? Quickly list your projects and deadlines, then consider the impact. Will accepting mean missing a deadline or working late again? This check helps avoid reflexively saying yes out of habit or fear.

If you realize you can't take on more work, it's time to communicate clearly and assertively. This isn't about making excuses or sounding defensive; it's about being honest and respectful to both yourself and your manager. Start by acknowledging the request: "I appreciate you thinking of me for this project." Then share the facts: "With my current deadlines for X and Y, I can't take this on without moving something else." Invite your boss to help set priorities: "Can you help me decide which project should come first?" This approach keeps the focus on results and your workload, not on personal shortcomings. It also shows you care about doing quality work, not just avoiding extra tasks.

Back up your refusal with facts to keep the conversation focused on practical details rather than feelings. Mention your current tasks and time required: "If I spend ten hours on this new assignment, our monthly report launch will be delayed." Offer options: "Which takes priority?" This shows you are solution-focused and makes the decision a team effort rather than a personal dispute.

If you worry about being called 'not a team player' or 'uncommitted,' you're not alone. Many women share this concern when setting boundaries. You might fear gossip or missing out, but people value clarity and consistency over constant availability. Research suggests women who link assertiveness to team results face less pushback. Try saying, "I'm committed to delivering my best. If I add this, something else will slip, and I want us to reach our goals," or, "Let's talk about this week's priorities so I can focus where it matters most."

Stand your ground while staying open and professional. Don't apologize for having limits; your time and energy deserve respect. If your supervisor pushes back, calmly restate your position: "I hear this is important. I want to support it, but these are my current capacities." Clear communication fosters a sense of safety and respect, empowering you to be assertive without guilt.

Your Boundary Blueprint at Work

Take a moment to think about the last time you felt overwhelmed by a request from your boss. Jot down:

- What was the request?

- How did you feel in your body, tension, anxiety, anger?

- Did you automatically say yes? Why?

- What would you say if you could do it over, using the scripts above?

- How can you use data (task lists, deadlines) next time to support your boundary?

Practice crafting two boundary statements: a gentle one like, "I'd love to help, but my current deadlines mean I can't take this on without moving something else," and a firmer one such as, "If I take this on, X and Y will be delayed. Which should be the priority?" As you read these aloud, notice how each feels in your mouth and body. This awareness helps you choose the most effective language for different situations, empowering you to communicate boundaries confidently.

Remember, setting boundaries at work not only protects your well-being but also empowers you to take control of your effectiveness, creativity, and focus. Being clear about your limits helps create healthier workplaces for everyone, making you feel more confident and in charge of your work life.

Group Chats, Slack, and After-Hours Texts, Protecting Your Off-the-Clock Time

The digital leash is real. Group chats buzz with 'urgent' questions at 9 pm, Slack messages pop up while you're folding laundry, and coworkers text before you've had your Saturday coffee. For women juggling careers, home life, and caregiving, this constant contact is overwhelming. The pressure to reply instantly, even outside work hours, causes anxiety or guilt.

This nonstop digital cycle erodes your downtime. Every after-hours 'quick question' intrudes on your free time. You might reply to avoid being seen as unhelpful or 'not dedicated.' Over time, these interruptions pile up, turning nights and weekends into unpaid work, hurting your creativity and mood.

You don't have to accept this digital overload as normal. Setting clear boundaries can reduce your anxiety and help you feel more relaxed outside work hours. Use friendly but firm scripts like: "I'm offline after 6 pm and will reply in the morning." These simple statements help you feel more in control and less overwhelmed.

Digital etiquette tools help. Set your Slack or Teams status to 'Away, responding tomorrow,' use auto-replies outside work hours, and block your calendar for personal time. These steps show that your time matters and help you keep boundaries. If your team overuses group chats, suggest, "Let's keep urgent after-hours needs to this number; otherwise, I'll see messages in the morning." Using these signals makes it easier to respect boundaries.

Proactive communication makes a difference. Discuss your digital boundaries in team meetings or during onboarding, not just when issues arise. You could say, "I'm making a habit of unplugging after work to stay focused. Unless it's urgent, I'll respond the next day." When new members join, set early expectations: "Our culture values work-life balance, so we keep messages during business hours." These conversations can be part of regular check-ins.

You might get pushback, especially if your company expects people to be available at all times or uses guilt to keep everyone online. Maybe a manager asks, "Did you see my message last night?" or a coworker jokes, "You're always missing after 6." These comments can hurt, but they're also a chance to stand by your values without getting defensive. Calmly reply with something like, "I want to make sure I'm fresh and productive, so I disconnect from work outside office hours." If someone says it's urgent, explain your process: "If it's truly an emergency, here's how to reach me; otherwise, I'll handle it first thing in the morning." This puts the responsibility back on the sender and helps protect your boundaries.

Company resistance can feel tough, especially where late-night emails are seen as a sign of dedication. If you notice a culture of quiet judgment or subtle pushback like, "We just assumed you wouldn't want to join this call," stick with your boundaries. Being consistent matters more than any single moment of pushback. Over time, people get used to clear, steady boundaries. If you need support, refer to research on productivity and burnout; many organizations now realize that tired employees aren't effective.

Digital Boundary Reset

Take five minutes now to audit your current digital availability:

- When do you usually check work messages after hours?

- How often do you respond immediately out of guilt or habit?

- What would an ideal after-hours routine look like for you?

Write one script you'll use this week to set a digital boundary with your team. Try it out in a real situation, notice how it feels in your body, and what reaction you get. If you get pushback, jot down what was said and how you want to respond next time.

Each time you reinforce your digital boundary, you make it easier to protect your time and energy. This practice benefits your peace of mind, energy, and happiness at work and in life.

Dealing with the Office Oversharer, Saying "That's Not My Job."

Work would be simpler if everyone stuck to their own responsibilities, but real life is messier. There's probably someone in your office, maybe more than one, who crosses professional boundaries often. You know the type: the coworker who shares her breakup story when you're on a deadline, the guy who asks you to cover his calls every Monday because he 'just can't focus today,' or the peer who expects you to listen to her weekend drama and then pick up her work when she leaves for a 'mental health walk.' At first, you might nod along or even feel flattered that they trust you. But over time, your patience wears thin and your own work piles up. Giving emotional support and taking on extra tasks starts to feel like unpaid overtime, and resentment builds.

People overshare or pass off work for many reasons. Sometimes it's just their personality, but often it's because they don't notice or respect boundaries. Women are often targeted because they're seen as 'nice,' good listeners, or the reliable ones who never say no. It might feel flattering at first, but it quickly becomes exhausting. You end up staying late to finish your own work after spending hours listening to someone else's crisis or doing tasks that aren't even part of your job. The pressure to be helpful while still meeting your real responsibilities can start to feel like a trap.

It's natural to want to keep the peace, especially if you want good relationships at work or want to avoid drama. But you don't have to take on everyone's stress or do work that isn't yours. Redirecting these situations might feel awkward at first, but it gets easier with practice and clear responses. If a coworker brings you more personal problems when you're busy, try saying, "I hope things get better for you, but I need to focus on this deadline." This shows you care without taking on their issues. If someone tries to give you tasks that aren't your job, be direct: "I'm not able to take this on; it's outside my responsibilities." This kind of language sets a clear boundary without making a big scene.

If coworkers often want to talk about personal matters at work, gentle redirection helps you maintain good relationships and protect your time. You can say, "Let's catch up about this at lunch or after work," or, "I want to stay focused right now, but I appreciate you sharing." These responses show you care without letting your productivity slip. If someone keeps talking, set a clear limit: "I'm happy to listen, but can we keep it brief so we both stay on track?" This shows you're practical and caring, and it helps you stand up for your priorities.

Some people will test your boundaries more than once. Speaking up once doesn't always lead to instant change. It helps to stay consistent and use neutral language, don't over-explain or justify yourself. The more straightforward you are, the less likely others are to get defensive or try to argue. If someone pushes back or complains, try not to fill the silence with apologies or extra explanations. Repeat your original statement if needed: "I really have to get back to this project right now." Most people will understand over time.

Sometimes, repeated boundary-crossing becomes a pattern. In these cases, it's smart to keep a simple record of what happens: note the dates, what was asked, how you responded, and any follow-up. This isn't about making trouble; it's about protecting yourself if things get worse or if you need help from HR. If someone keeps giving you tasks that aren't yours, even after you say no, send a polite but clear follow-up email: "Just confirming that I won't be able to cover X as discussed earlier today. Please let me know if there's any confusion." This gives you a written record and helps avoid misunderstandings.

If things get more difficult, like ongoing pressure or retaliation, you may need to bring the issue to official channels. Having documentation makes it much easier to explain your side to HR or management. You can use an email like: "Hi [Manager/HR], I wanted to make sure expectations are clear regarding my responsibilities. Over the past month, I've received several requests from [Colleague] to handle tasks outside my role. I've communicated my limits directly, but wanted to document this pattern for future reference." Keep your message professional and stick to the facts; don't vent or add personal opinions.

You don't have to pick between being kind and having boundaries; you can have both. By using neutral, direct language and keeping records when needed, you protect your job performance and your peace of mind. Colleagues might not always thank you for setting limits, but your future self will be glad for every moment you save for important work and every bit of energy you keep for life outside the office.

Handling Backlash, When Colleagues Weaponize Guilt or Exclusion

Few things sting as sharply as realizing you've become the office scapegoat just for having limits. Maybe you didn't volunteer for a last-minute project or declined another "quick favor." Suddenly, the air shifts, side-eyes in the break room, your name missing from meeting invites, group lunches planned without you. Subtle comments follow: "You're not much of a team player these days," or "We assumed you wouldn't want to be involved." There's no direct attack, only enough to spark self-doubt and make you question whether advocating for yourself was a mistake.

This backlash is especially harsh for women, who often face unspoken or explicit pressure to remain agreeable. Colleagues may rely on passive-aggressive tactics, whispers about your "attitude," or awkward pauses when you enter a room. When you set boundaries in an environment that rewards overextension, guilt-tripping emerges: "We could use your skills, but I guess you're busy," or "Some people just don't want to pitch in." The aim is the same: to pull you back into unhealthy patterns and undermine your right to protect your time and energy.

It's easy to shrink away or over-explain, but you don't have to accept exclusion or indirect hostility. When you notice you've been left out of a meeting, project, or even a coffee run, address it directly but calmly: "I noticed I wasn't included, was that intentional?" This invites honest conversation and signals your awareness and engagement. If exclusion persists, reinforce your stance: "I value being part of the team and want to stay informed." Or clarify your commitment: "I'm dedicated, even if I can't take on extra tasks." Such statements are direct, not confrontational, and remind others of your value without labeling you as disengaged.

Follow-up can be crucial. If anyone makes a snide remark about your boundaries in front of others, speak with them privately later: "I sensed some frustration earlier about my availability. I care about our work and am open to feedback." This approach defuses tension and shifts the conversation from public shaming to private resolution. If exclusion continues, document each incident with dates and details in a private log, which can be valuable if you need to escalate matters.

Workplace culture too often rewards people who continually overextend themselves. Remember, you're not alone in facing backlash for setting limits. One of the most effective defenses is building alliances. Seek out colleagues who also value fairness and respect, and notice who else appears exhausted by people-pleasing expectations. Allies may seem quiet at first, but will often support you if asked directly. Start by checking in: "Have you noticed changes in meetings lately?" or, "I've felt out of the loop, has that happened to you?" Honest conversations are how solidarity begins.

If your boundaries are continually ignored or weaponized against you, it might be time to reach out to mentors, HR, or affinity groups (like women's networks or employee resource groups). When approaching HR, stick to neutral, fact-based language: "I'd like some guidance on maintaining inclusion after setting new workload limits." In private check-ins, express yourself clearly: "I want to stay involved and productive. How do I navigate this dynamic?" Mentors can share strategies and help you practice your responses.

Addressing exclusion and guilt-tripping isn't just about changing others; it's also about protecting your own mental health. Here, self-care is essential. After tough interactions, give yourself a moment to breathe or step outside. Repeat simple affirmations: "Protecting my time is professional, not selfish." Or, "I am still valuable even when I say no." Even a short walk or jotting down your thoughts can help reset your mindset and stop slights from morphing into self-doubt.

No matter how much pushback you get, setting boundaries shows strength, not weakness. Every time you stand firm, even if you face gossip or feel left out, you reinforce your self-worth and show that you don't need anyone's approval to respect yourself. The people who matter will notice, and sometimes even those who resisted at first will respect your limits when they see you doing well instead of burning out.

As this chapter ends, remember that healthy boundaries at work protect more than just your schedule; they also guard your energy, creativity, and sense of fairness. Pushback can hurt, but standing firm helps you build resilience that lasts beyond any one team or project. Next, we'll look at how emotional resilience can strengthen your boundaries and help you thrive on your own terms.

Chapter Seven

Romantic Boundaries, Balancing Intimacy and Independence

I Need Spacc: How to Ask for Alone Time Without Starting a Fight

Imagine sitting with your partner on the couch, feeling pressured when you crave a few hours alone to read, take a walk, or enjoy quiet. Worrying about how to ask for that space can lead to guilt. Society often expects couples to be together all the time, but needing time apart isn't a sign of trouble. Taking time for yourself is a healthy way to care for yourself and your relationship.

It's a common myth that wanting alone time means you love your partner less or that something is wrong in your relationship. The belief that real love means always being together just isn't realistic for most people. Sometimes, cultural expectations, especially for women, make it feel selfish to ask for space if you grew up where being together was expected. But spending time alone helps you recharge; it doesn't mean you're shutting your partner out.

Spending time alone is good for you. It lets you recharge so you can bring more energy and attention to your relationship. Recognizing that everyone's need for connection and space can change helps keep your relationship close and healthy, preventing it from feeling too tight or dependent. It's like regular maintenance for your relationship, giving both people space to breathe and grow.

It's normal to feel nervous about asking for space. Be gentle, honest, and clear, so your audience feels understood and supported. You can say: "I love spending time with you, but I also need a solo recharge tonight." "This isn't about us having problems; I just need time for myself." "Alone time makes me more energized and excited to see you." Or keep it warm and direct: "I care about you, and alone time helps me be my best self."

Share your needs with confidence. You don't have to apologize too much or explain yourself. Reassure your partner and your audience: "Needing space doesn't mean something is wrong." "I want us strong together, and having time for myself is part of that." "This actually makes me come back to our relationship feeling refreshed and happy."

You don't have to fix every uncomfortable feeling your partner has, but you can show you care by warmly checking in: "How are you feeling about this? Is anything on your mind?" Talking about worries together can help your audience feel more secure and less isolated, easing tension.

If your partner gets defensive or hurt, it's often because they see closeness as always being together. Stay calm and say, "I understand this feels hard for you. Space grounds me; it's not about pulling away." Gently keep expressing your need, and try to stay warm but firm.

If asking for space leads to arguments, propose regular "me time" for both of you, like solo walks or nights with friends. Making it routine normalizes independence. For example: "How about we both take Thursday evenings for ourselves? Then we'll have new stories to share."

Your Alone Time Blueprint

Think of three times you wanted time alone but felt guilty asking for it. What held you back? What were you afraid might happen? Next, write a short, natural script for how you'd share your need. For each one, add a line to reassure your partner that this is about self-care, not pulling away. For example: "I've realized I get overwhelmed without quiet time after work. Taking an hour for myself helps me be kinder and more present with you." As you write, notice how you feel: tense, relieved, or worried, and let those feelings guide your future conversations.

If things feel tense after you ask for space, suggest checking in when you're back together. You might say, "Let's talk about how we each felt during our solo time." Encourage both of you to be honest. This helps build trust and prevents resentment.

Personal space isn't a luxury; it's necessary for a healthy relationship where both people can thrive. Setting and talking about boundaries around alone time shows self-respect and helps your relationship grow on a real connection, not silent sacrifice.

Money, Chores, and "Invisible Labor" Negotiating Fairness at Home

Money and chores can strain even happy relationships, especially if work isn't shared fairly. Resentment can build quietly; maybe you're always doing laundry, paying bills, or planning birthdays and appointments without thanks. This is invisible labor: the mental and emotional effort that keeps things running, often unnoticed. It includes remembering deadlines, making grocery lists, checking on family, and ensuring everything at home runs smoothly. If you're the only one keeping track, it's exhausting and lonely.

Discussing fairness at home can feel tough. You may worry your partner will feel hurt or misunderstood. But staying quiet builds frustration and leads to petty arguments. Be open and gentle. Say, "Can we work on chores together to make it fair?" or "Let's review our budget." Use "I" statements, like, "I'm handling most laundry and feel overwhelmed." This builds teamwork and understanding.

When you talk about who does what, make it clear by writing everything down. List all regular tasks, such as dishes, trash, laundry, pet care, bills, meals, holiday planning, and emotional support. You might be surprised by how much you do. Ask your partner to add to the list, then discuss how to share the work fairly, such as by switching weeks or dividing by preference. Use chore charts or shared apps like Google Calendar to stay organized.

Money can create more stress, especially if you grew up with arguments or taboos about it. Not talking leads to mismatched expectations. Start gently: "I want us both to be secure with money. Can we review our budget?" Be open about who pays for what, about savings, about extra spending, and about big decisions. If incomes change, discuss what feels fair instead of sticking to old routines or feeling guilty.

Invisible labor is harder to spot because it's often about mental and emotional work. Use checklists for this, too: Who remembers birthdays? Who makes appointments? Who keeps everyone updated? If you're doing most of these things, bring it up: "I feel like I'm juggling a lot of behind-the-scenes stuff, and I'd love for us to share that more." Sometimes, people don't notice these tasks unless you point them out.

Your living situation affects these conversations. Couples who live together might need regular check-ins to adjust chores. Long-distance couples may split costs differently and need to talk directly and use digital tools. Blended families face unique challenges, such as working with ex-partners and managing stepkids' routines. Clear communication and simple scripts help, like, "Let's agree on a pickup calendar," or "Can we talk about sharing chores with the kids?" With exes, stay neutral: "I'll handle groceries this week if you take next week's activities."

If you start feeling resentful again, gently share the details and how you feel. For example, "Last month I did laundry 12 times and cooked 20 dinners. I'm feeling tired and a bit unappreciated." This isn't about keeping score; it's about showing your partner the work you do so they can understand how it affects you.

To help, try using chore chart templates or apps like *Cozi* or *OurHome* to track tasks together. Check in and update them each week; the system doesn't have to be perfect, just open and consistent. If you have stepchildren or new routines, make expectations clear: "Everyone puts their own dishes away," or "We'll rotate trash duty." Scripts can help here too: "I want everyone pitching in so no one feels overloaded."

Shared calendars save time and lower stress. Sync schedules to avoid missed appointments or overwhelm. Try Google Calendar, Outlook, or a dry-erase board to keep things visible.

Fairness at home doesn't require perfection. What matters is having open conversations, noticing when things get out of balance, and raising problems early to avoid resentment. Both partners should feel noticed and supported, including for the mental work. This strengthens your relationship and keeps resentment low. Arguments about chores and money aren't disasters; they're chances to build a better partnership.

Key takeaways:

1) Open communication helps prevent misunderstandings and resentment.

2) Recognize and support both the visible tasks and the unseen mental load.

3) View conflict or tension as an opportunity to discuss concerns and create shared solutions that improve your relationship.

Chore Chart Template

Set up three columns, and fill it out together.

Task – Who Does It Now – Who Next Week
Dishes
Laundry
Meals
Trash
Groceries
Appointments

Update and post it somewhere visible. Then, review it together each week and adjust as needed.

Fairness doesn't just happen by accident; it comes from honest, practical conversations. To create a fair home, talk about your needs, suggest solutions, and invite your partner to work with you on them. This way, invisible work becomes visible, and you build more care and teamwork.

Handling Love Bombing, Gaslighting, and Codependency

Sometimes, what seems like deep devotion is actually a pattern of manipulation. It can drain your energy, lower your confidence, and make you doubt yourself. Love bombing, gaslighting, and codependency can sneak into relationships, especially if you're looking for connection or surprised by someone's intensity. These are real problems, not just buzzwords. You might notice them if you've ever been swept up by too much affection or attention that feels almost unreal. Love bombing often means big gestures, expensive gifts, or constant contact early on. At first, it feels exciting and special, but soon you might feel pressured, your partner wants all your time, expects instant closeness, or gets jealous when you set even a small boundary.

Gaslighting is subtler and more insidious. It's not just lying; it's someone making you doubt your own memories or feelings. You might hear, "You're imagining things, I never said that," or "You always overreact." Eventually, you start replaying conversations in your head, doubting your judgment, and apologizing for things you never did. What was once certainty about your needs can turn to confusion and self-blame.

Codependency has its own challenges. You might notice it if you're always putting your partner first and ignoring your own needs. Maybe you try to fix everything when your partner is upset. Helping can feel good, but if your mood depends on theirs, or you feel responsible for making them happy, something isn't right. You might even feel guilty for wanting something different.

Being able to spot these behaviors as they happen is important. If you notice warning signs, like too much affection too soon, let yourself slow things down. You can say, "I need to slow things down so I can feel comfortable." This isn't rude, it's about taking care of yourself.

If you're dealing with gaslighting, try not to argue about every detail; it can make things worse. Instead, stick to your own experience. You can say, "When you say I'm overreacting, it makes me doubt myself," or, "I remember it differently." You don't have to convince them; what matters is trusting yourself. If your partner keeps acting this way, calmly repeat your point instead of getting stuck in arguments.

If you notice codependency, like always doing emotional work or feeling responsible for your partner's happiness, talk about it openly. You can say, "I love you, but I can't be responsible for your happiness." This doesn't mean it's honest. Real love doesn't mean losing yourself in someone else's problems.

Sometimes, even after you talk about these patterns, the manipulation continues. If your boundaries are ignored or apologies don't stop the hurtful behavior, it's time to seek support outside the relationship. Friends and family can often see changes in you before you do. Therapists and support groups can give you a helpful perspective that's hard to find when you're in the middle of things. If you notice you're always anxious, walking on eggshells, or feeling smaller, pay attention to those signs.

Some warning signs mean it might be safest to think about leaving, especially if the manipulation gets worse, you feel unsafe emotionally or physically, or respect never returns, no matter what you do. No one deserves to feel invisible, controlled, or always blamed.

Spotting Your Patterns

Grab a notebook or use your phone. Write: "When do I feel most anxious in this relationship?" Be honest, maybe it's after arguments, extravagant gifts, or when you try to state a need and get dismissed. Use this checklist:

- Do I feel pressured to move faster than I want?

- Do I question my memory after disagreements?

- Do I say "yes" to keep the peace?

- Have I stopped seeing friends or doing things I love?

- Is my mood tied to my partner's more than my own?

- Do I feel responsible for fixing everything?

If several of these fit, take notice. This isn't about blaming anyone; it's about looking after your own well-being.

These patterns are more common than most people admit. The bravest thing you can do is name what's happening and trust that your needs are important. Boundaries aren't walls; they're a way to say, "I matter here too."

When Your Partner's Family Pushes In, Holiday Scripts and Default Defenses

Few things test your patience like your partner's family crossing boundaries, especially during holidays or big events. Plans you thought were yours can suddenly include in-laws' opinions, surprise visits, and pressure to go to every gathering, no matter what you want. You might get advice you didn't ask for about decorating, parenting, or celebrating, or hear guilt trips like, "But it's tradition," or "Everyone is expecting you." It can leave you feeling like your home and time aren't really yours.

These situations can make you feel torn. You want to support your partner, but you also need to feel in control of your own life. Many people worry that setting boundaries will upset others, cause drama, or put their partner in a tough spot. Often, women hold back their needs to keep the peace, leading to quiet resentment. This isn't about being unkind; it's about being human and needing space. Old family habits can come back quickly, especially when traditions are involved.

To avoid stress, talk with your partner before the holidays or big events. Discuss what feels right for both of you before making plans with others. Ask open, honest questions like, "Can we talk about how your family's holiday plans fit with ours?" or, "What would feel good to us this year?" Work as a team. Share your preferences and limits clearly; maybe you want Christmas morning alone, or you want to alternate holidays between families. Listen to your partner's feelings too; they might also feel overwhelmed and need your support. Deciding together makes it easier to handle outside pressure.

Once you've agreed on a plan, show a united front to your extended family. Decide together what you'll say, when you'll say it, and who will deliver the message. If relatives push, keep your answers short but kind: "Thank you for thinking of us, but we're spending this holiday just the two of us." If people give opinions about recipes, guest lists, or traditions, you can say, "We appreciate your advice, but we've decided to do things our own way this year." These answers might feel awkward at first, but they're polite and clear. Don't apologize for setting boundaries; you don't have to explain that you want a peaceful holiday.

If you get pushback, disappointment, or emotional pleas like, "But we always do it this way," stay calm and steady. Repeat your boundary almost exactly. People sometimes test limits to see if you'll give in. If a gathering gets tense, or someone corners you about plans, have a private "safe word" with your partner to signal you need help or a break. This helps you both step away or change the subject before things get worse.

To stay calm before and after family events, create some self-care habits. Before gatherings, take a few deep breaths or go for a short walk, and remind yourself it's okay if not everyone agrees with your choices. Afterward, check in with your partner: "How did that feel for you? Should we change anything for next time?" These talks help you both process feelings and adjust boundaries without blaming each other.

If someone crosses your boundaries, like showing up without warning or trying to guilt you into changing plans, respond calmly but firmly. You can say, "We weren't expecting company today; next time, please call first," or "We've already made other plans." Standing your ground now helps set expectations for the future. If it gets to be too much, it's okay to excuse yourself, step outside, take a few minutes alone, or find a quiet spot to regroup.

Remember, taking care of yourself in these situations isn't selfish; it's necessary. Whether you limit your time at events or plan some downtime afterward, do what helps you recharge and stay present. Sometimes, the best plan is to have an exit strategy: drive separately so you can leave when you need to, or schedule something afterward as a reason to step away.

Holidays and special events can show where family boundaries need work, but they're also a chance to set new expectations and healthier ways to connect. When you and your partner stand together and share your needs kindly and clearly, you protect your peace and your relationship.

In short, a real partnership means making room for both closeness and independence, not just with each other, but with everyone in your life. Setting boundaries with extended family can be tough, but it's important for stronger relationships and less resentment later on. Next, we'll talk about how to keep your boundaries even when things get difficult and people push back.

Chapter Eight

Emotional Resilience, Managing Guilt, Anxiety, and Pushback

Why The Guilt Spiral Happens and How to Break Free

You know that feeling after you say "no." Your chest tightens. A voice tells you you're letting someone down. The moment replays in your mind, filled with what-ifs and self-doubt, making you question whether setting boundaries is worth it. For many women, guilt shadows every attempt to separate self-care from caring for others. Much of this guilt isn't yours alone. It's passed down, taught, and reinforced by a society that expects you always to nurture, keep the peace, and never let others down. Recognizing this can help you feel understood and less isolated in your experience.

Since childhood, you've learned what it means to be "good." Maybe you did chores or felt pressure to agree, hearing, "Don't be difficult," or "Family comes first." Over time, these lessons create an invisible rulebook measuring your value by how much you give and how smoothly you keep things moving. As you age, culture reinforces this: movies, social media, and family suggest that being needed is best. If you step outside that role, guilt follows.

This pressure goes beyond tradition. It shapes your thoughts and feelings. Society praises women who notice and meet others' needs but quietly criticizes those who speak up. If you wonder, "What will they think of me?" after setting a boundary, it's not a flaw; it's a learned behavior. These feelings linger. You may feel doubt after turning down an invitation, asking for help, or refusing extra work. They're meant to keep you in line, not support your well-being.

How can you tell if your guilt is healthy or harmful? Clarifying this helps women recognize when guilt supports boundaries or when it's a sign of self-sabotage. Healthy guilt arises when you've truly hurt someone and urges you to make amends. Toxic guilt appears when you've protected yourself. It calls you selfish just for saying no. Unlike healthy guilt, toxic guilt doesn't stem from a real mistake; it comes from old habits and social pressure.

"What's the Story Behind My Guilt?"

Try this exercise: After you feel guilty for setting a boundary, write down your thoughts. Whose voice do you hear, maybe a parent, a boss, or society? List three recent times you felt guilty after saying no. For each one, ask yourself: Did I actually hurt someone, or did I go against what was expected? Notice if certain people or situations make you feel more guilty.

Example chart:

Scenario - Healthy Guilt (actual harm?) - Toxic Guilt (just saying no?)
Skipped niece's birthday party - No - Yes
Forgot best friend's birthday - Yes - No
Said no to extra work on weekend - No - Yes

When you realize that most of your guilt comes from simply saying no, it's time to question the rules you're following.

To break the guilt spiral, try three steps: name it, normalize it, and neutralize it. Start by naming your guilt, write it down, or say it out loud, like, "I feel guilty for turning down Sunday dinner." Naming the feeling makes it less powerful. Next, normalize it by reminding yourself that many women feel this way; you're not alone, and it's not a flaw. This can help you feel validated and less overwhelmed by your emotions. Finally, neutralize the guilt by asking, "Is my boundary unfair?" or "Did I hurt anyone?" If the answer is no, remind yourself, "I have a right to my limits."

Create a brief script to interrupt guilt early, such as, "This feels uncomfortable because it's new, not because it's wrong," or, "I'm allowed to care for myself." Developing and practicing this script helps women respond to guilt with confidence, reinforcing emotional resilience. Keeping this script handy helps prevent guilt from growing, empowering women to set boundaries without feeling overwhelmed.

Think of three times you set a boundary, whether big or small, and nothing bad happened. Maybe you skipped an event, and everyone was fine with it. Or you said no to covering a shift, and things still worked out. Write these examples down. Remind yourself that setting boundaries doesn't lead to disaster.

Try writing a kind letter from your future self. Picture yourself five years from now, stronger, more relaxed, thriving because you respected your needs. Let your future self reassure you: "It was scary at first, but I'm grateful you protected us. Saying no made space for what matters." This exercise might feel odd. It helps your mind expect growth instead of disaster. With awareness and practice, guilt loses its grip. Each time you reflect instead of react, use your script, or gather proof that boundaries don't ruin relationships, you weaken old habits. You're not betraying anyone by putting your well-being first. You're simply creating a new idea of what it means to be "good" for yourself and for those who love the real you."

The Anxiety Toolkit, Grounding Techniques for Tough Conversations

Your body often feels stress before your mind notices it. You might have a racing heart, sweaty palms, chest tightness, or an upset stomach. Your thoughts may start to spiral, and you might imagine things going badly, like anger, silence, or tears. These reactions aren't weaknesses. They are normal ways your body responds to things that feel risky or unfamiliar, especially if you've spent years trying to keep the peace or avoid conflict.

These signals are signs of anxiety. This is your body's way of protecting you. When you face something stressful, such as a hard conversation or the fear of letting someone down, your nervous system reacts with "fight, flight, or freeze." You might get defensive, want to leave, or feel stuck. These responses are just how you're wired. They don't mean anything is wrong with you. The important thing is to calm yourself enough to stay present and speak up, even if you'd rather avoid it.

Before a tough conversation, prepare grounding techniques. Grounding helps you focus and respond thoughtfully. Try the 4-7-8 breathing method: inhale for 4 counts, hold for 7 counts, exhale for 8 counts. This relaxes your nervous system and quiets your mind. Repeat before or during the conversation. No one needs to notice.

Another helpful tool is "boundary breathing." As you inhale, draw in courage. As you exhale, let go of tension. Add a calming phrase, such as "I am safe. I can handle this." A mantra changes your self-talk and prevents panic. For a more subtle method, press your thumb and forefinger together and focus on the sensation. This small action grounds you without anyone noticing.

If a boundary conversation feels tough, try a simple ritual before you begin. Use this checklist:

- Affirmations: Remind yourself, "My needs matter," or "I have a right to speak up."

- Music: Play music that soothes or empowers you.

- Visualize a positive outcome: See yourself staying calm, speaking clearly, and finishing proud.

- Physically reset: Roll your shoulders back, stand tall, or shake out your hands.

The goal isn't to eliminate anxiety, but to lower it so you can be yourself. Rituals shift your focus to something helpful rather than worries.

If anxiety rises in a conversation or someone reacts badly, emotions can overwhelm. Allow yourself to pause. Say, "I need a moment to collect my thoughts," or, "This matters to me, and I want to be clear. Can we take a short break?" If needed, repeat, "I need a second." Expressing your needs gives your body time to calm down. You aren't avoiding the issue.

If you feel yourself spiraling, your heart racing, and words stuck, try grounding yourself in the present. Notice how the chair feels, your feet on the floor, or the temperature of the air. You can also list five things you see or three sounds you hear.

When you fear confrontation or feel like shutting down, keep a favorite grounding tool nearby. Use a sticky note or set a phone reminder. These prompts can help when panic starts.

Pre-Conversation Ritual

- **Affirmations:** Write three honest affirmations for today.

- **Music:** Pick a song that calms or energizes you.

- **Visualization:** Imagine yourself speaking calmly and clearly.

- **Physical Reset:** Roll your shoulders back, unclench your jaw, and stretch your hands.

- **Grounding Object:** Bring a small item (like a stone or ring) to touch if you feel anxious.

Having these tools ready means you won't scramble if anxiety hits. You'll know what grounds you. That way, you can maintain your boundaries calmly.

When emotions are strong, remember anxiety appears because you care. What you're doing is important, not just for others, but for yourself. Each time you ground yourself and speak up, even if your voice shakes, you build self-trust. Over time, anxiety's physical signs become less scary. They remind you of your growth.

Reframing "Selfishness" From Self-Sacrifice to Self-Respect

You've probably heard it, or felt it, at least once: "You're being selfish." It's the accusation that echoes in a woman's mind the second she dares to say, "I can't do that," or, "I need something different." It's almost as if the world has a script ready whenever a woman chooses herself. This idea didn't just show up in our generation. For centuries, women's self-advocacy has been painted as a flaw, a threat, or a reason for shame. If you look back, even early psychology pathologized women who asserted needs or boundaries; words like "hysteria" got thrown around for women who spoke up. Feminist thinkers have pointed out how society has long rewarded women for self-sacrifice and punished them for standing their ground. It's not surprising that, even now, "selfish" is one of the sharpest arrows in the quiver of anyone threatened by your limits.

But here's what people often miss: setting boundaries isn't about taking more than your share or putting yourself first at others' expense. It's about respecting your own worth just as much as anyone else's. The old idea says your needs should come last, as if it's noble to run on empty. That story isn't true. Every time you say no to something that drains you, or yes to something that helps you, you're not being unkind; you're honoring yourself and those around you. You make sure what you give is genuine, not forced or resentful.

When you start to see "selfish" as "self-respecting," things change. Think about the difference between someone who says yes because she truly wants to, and someone who says yes because she feels she has no choice. The first comes from real care; the second leads to resentment or burnout. You deserve to change that inner story. Instead of thinking, "I'm asking for too much," try saying, "My needs matter as much as anyone's." It may feel strange at first, but repeating it, especially when you doubt yourself, helps it become true for you.

Visualization can help you hold onto this new way of thinking. Imagine boundaries as a gentle hand on your shoulder, reminding you that you're allowed to be comfortable in your own life. Picture saying no, not as closing a door, but as opening a window for fresh air, letting in what helps you and letting out what doesn't. When you keep your boundaries with kindness, you show your kids, friends, and coworkers that it's possible to be both caring and clear.

People may still throw the word "selfish" at you when you set a limit they don't like. This is often about their discomfort with change, not the morality of your choices. When that happens, having tools ready to challenge those accusations is powerful. Practice a "script swap" exercise: take a negative label, "selfish," "difficult," "mean," and find its positive reframe. Write it out:

- "Selfish" becomes "self-aware" or "self-respecting."

- "Difficult" becomes "direct."

- "Mean" becomes "honest."

Say these new labels out loud, or write them down on your phone so you have them ready when you face criticism. You can also use responses like, "I care about our relationship, which is why I'm being clear," or "Taking care of myself helps me support others better." If someone says you're letting them down, remind yourself that their disappointment is real, but it doesn't mean you did something wrong.

A powerful way to see the impact of self-respect is through real stories. For example, my friend started saying no to last-minute requests in her group chat. At first, she felt anxious and worried about losing friends. But instead, a few women reached out privately to say they admired her courage and admitted they wanted to set limits too, but were nervous. Her honesty encouraged others to do the same, and soon the group began scheduling with more respect for everyone's time.

Another example is a colleague who used to take on everyone's extra work until she started setting clear boundaries about her workload. At first, people pushed back. Some tried to guilt-trip her or made comments about her dedication, but she stayed calm and respectful. Over time, others noticed she wasn't burning out anymore; she was more focused, less stressed, and even had energy for team lunches again. Soon, another coworker started protecting her own lunch break, inspired by her example.

These stories aren't about just changing one person's experience; they show how boundary-setting can shift whole communities toward healthier dynamics. When you honor yourself with clear limits, you invite others to do the same. You teach your kids that their feelings matter; you show friends you can love them without losing yourself; you help colleagues see that balance is possible, even in tough environments.

If you find yourself stuck in old beliefs, like thinking self-sacrifice is the cost of love, try changing your self-talk every day for a week. When guilt or fear shows up after you say no, pause and repeat: "Taking care of myself protects my relationships." Picture yourself moving through life with quiet confidence, knowing that self-respect supports everything good you give to others.

Setting boundaries doesn't make you less caring; it creates space for real connection and joy. The idea that boundaries are selfish is just a myth meant to keep women quiet and agreeable. You can choose a new story now, one where self-care and caring for others go together, and where respecting yourself shapes every relationship you have.

"Am I the Drama?" Managing Fear of Rejection and Relationship Fallout

It's normal to wonder, "Am I the drama?" when setting boundaries causes tension. You might worry, Will they be upset? Will this ruin our relationship? If you grew up trying to keep the peace or were ever called "too much" for speaking up, conflict can feel scary. It's understandable to fear being seen as difficult, selfish, or cold when you finally share your needs. Even the most confident person can second-guess herself, replaying conversations and looking for signs she went too far.

This fear, while uncomfortable, shows that you care about your relationships and how others see you. It comes from the social risks women face when they stop being agreeable. Society and history reward women for being accommodating, but when you challenge that, people may pull away. Most people feel this anxiety when they start setting boundaries; it's a normal part of the process, not a personal flaw.

You don't have to let this fear control your choices. Building courage isn't about getting rid of discomfort; it's about becoming more comfortable with awkward or uncertain moments. Think of it like climbing a ladder. At the bottom are small boundaries, like saying no to coffee or asking to finish a task before chatting; these are low-risk. As you get used to it, you move up to bigger boundaries, like asking for quiet at home, saying no to extra work, or being less available to a friend who wants to vent. Eventually, you'll handle high-stakes boundaries, such as discussing money or major responsibilities. Each step makes you more confident.

You don't need to start with the hardest boundary. Pick something small and practice staying steady, even if it feels awkward. It's not about being perfect, but about getting used to discomfort and seeing that it won't harm you. Over time, what once felt overwhelming will become just another situation you know how to handle.

When things get tense, clear and direct communication helps. You can say, "I know this is uncomfortable, but I want us to be honest with each other," or, "I'm not trying to hurt you, but I need to be clear about my limits." These phrases show you care and set the stage for a real conversation, making it clear your boundaries aren't a rejection or punishment, but an honest exchange.

If someone reacts with drama, like raising their voice, sulking, or snapping, being clear is important. You can calmly say, "This feels tense right now, but I hope we can get through it together." Standing by your words without attacking or apologizing too much helps others learn how to interact with you, even if it takes them time to adjust.

After a tough conversation or a negative reaction, it's normal to feel shaky or regretful. This is when your personal care plan matters. Soothe yourself with tea, a favorite show, music, or a walk. Think of this as recovery, not wasted time; you did something brave. Give yourself time to process, without judging yourself.

Journaling helps sort out emotions or doubts. Note what went well, maybe you stayed calm or didn't backpedal, and what was hard. Ask, "What would I keep the same? What might I do differently?" This practice isn't about self-criticism, but collecting insights for future situations. Over time, these reflections show tangible proof of your growth.

Don't overlook your wins, even if things didn't go perfectly. Honor your courage for being true to yourself. Small acts of self-kindness, like enjoying a favorite snack, talking to a supportive friend, or lighting a candle, remind you that your progress is worth celebrating.

The worry about being "the drama" might never disappear completely, but it gets weaker as you see that real relationships can handle honesty and boundaries. Some relationships will grow stronger, while others may fade, and that's normal. The more you practice being true to yourself, even when it's uncomfortable, the more resilient and confident you'll become.

Conflict isn't always a disaster; it can lead to more understanding and respect, even if it's just from yourself. As this chapter comes to an end, remember that facing your fears is part of real change. Boundaries might cause some discomfort, but the peace and self-respect you gain are worth it.

Next, we'll explore how to maintain strong boundaries and adjust them as your life changes.

Chapter Nine

Troubleshooting & Repair, When Boundaries Are Ignored or Broken

The Boundary Violator's Playbook For Recognizing Manipulation Tactics

Have you ever left a conversation feeling unsettled or doubting yourself for wanting simple things, like time alone or fair treatment at work? That feeling and the thought, "Am I the problem?" can be signs of someone using tactics from the boundary violator's playbook. Recognizing these patterns is important. Once you see them, you'll spot them everywhere. Becoming aware swaps self-doubt for clarity and confidence.

Let's look at common ways people push your boundaries. Guilt-tripping sounds caring but aims to make you feel bad: "After all I've done for you, how could you say no?" or "If you really cared, you'd help." Gaslighting makes you question your memory or feelings: "I never said that," or "You're overreacting." Triangulation uses others to pressure: "Your sister never complains." Playing the victim gets your sympathy, so you drop your boundary: "I guess I can't do anything right." Love bombing is sudden praise or gifts to make you feel off balance. Stonewalling means ignoring your request or giving you the silent treatment. Persistent "testing" is repeatedly pushing your boundary in small ways.

You've likely run into these behaviors: maybe a friend repeatedly calls late at night, or a coworker doubts your commitment when you say no to extra work. Sometimes a parent says, "You never really cared about this family," when you set a limit. These actions are often ways to push back against your new boundaries.

Manipulation Red Flags

Here's a quick self-check for tough moments when you doubt yourself:

- Do I feel confused, guilty, or pressured?

- Is someone using the past or others to sway me?

- Did their tone shift when I said no?

- Am I being blamed for their mood?

- Are my needs suddenly "too much" or "selfish"?

- Is there always a crisis when I try to step back?

If you answer yes to any, pause and notice: "That's guilt-tripping," or "They're making me doubt myself." Remind yourself that just because someone is upset doesn't mean you're wrong, and their discomfort doesn't make your boundary unfair. It's okay to disappoint others.

It takes practice to avoid manipulation. Try a micro-boundary, a short, clear statement like "Let's stick to the present," or "I need a break from this conversation." These aren't rude; they're assertive ways to protect your peace. Remember, setting boundaries assertively is different from being aggressive or dismissive, which can harm relationships and hinder your goal of improving emotional health.

If something feels off, step back to protect yourself. You don't need anyone else's approval to stand up for your boundaries. Trusting your judgment builds confidence and resilience in managing relationships.

Manipulation can be hard to spot and may look different each time-guilt one day, silence the next, or sudden emotional outbursts. Recognizing these warning signs early helps you respond effectively. The more you notice these patterns, the less power they have over you. Use this checklist until spotting warning signs feels natural. Now, take the next step: here's what to do when someone ignores your boundaries, especially if the violation escalates.

What to Do When Someone Ignores Your Boundary, Step-by-Step Escalation

When someone ignores your boundary, you might freeze or doubt yourself, especially if they're close to you. You could feel angry, confused, or guilty, or wonder if you explained things badly. Usually, repeated boundary violations aren't about how you said it; they're about the other person not respecting your needs. That's why having a plan for what to do next can help you stay calm and in control.

Step one: Restate your boundary calmly and clearly. The goal is to remind the other person of your needs without apologizing or seeking permission. For family: "As I mentioned, I can't commit to Sunday dinners every week." At work: "As I said earlier, I'm unavailable after hours." With friends: "I can't always be the one to drive." In romance: "I need alone time in the evenings." State your boundary as a fact to set a respectful tone.

Step two: If your boundary is still not honored, clearly explain the consequences of continued violations. The goal here is to set direct expectations for what you will do if the pattern continues, so the other person understands what will happen next. For example: "If this keeps happening, I'll have to reconsider how often we see each other." Or, "If you keep calling after 8 p.m., I'll start turning my phone off." At work: "If late tasks continue, I'll only respond during work hours." In romance: "If my need for space isn't respected, I'll spend more nights at my own place." Make sure your consequence is specific and directly stated.

Step three: If the person still crosses your boundary, follow through with the consequences you stated. This step is about consistency; taking action shows you are serious and reinforces your boundary. For example: "Because you kept calling late, I won't be answering tonight." With family: "Since my request wasn't respected, I'll only visit once a month now." At work: "I'll answer after-hours requests during work time only." Friendship: "Since my wishes weren't honored, I need to take a step back from our usual plans." Following through prevents your boundaries from being undermined.

Step four: If you have used clear boundaries and consequences and nothing changes, limit or end contact as needed. This step is necessary to protect your well-being when less drastic steps have failed. For the family, it might mean fewer visits or only attending group events. In friendships or romantic relationships, it could mean taking a break or ending things. At work, this can mean reducing unnecessary interactions or escalating to HR when communication fails. If you reach this stage, keep your message simple: "I need distance right now for my well-being," or "This dynamic isn't working for me."

Track your boundaries, especially if things get emotional or you need help, such as from HR or a mediator. Note the date, what you said or did, what the other person did, and their response. For example: "April 3, Set a boundary about no late calls with Mom. April 7, she called at midnight; I reminded her." At work: "May 1, told manager I don't reply after 6 p.m. May 2, got three emails at 8 p.m.; replied the next day." Recording events helps you stay clear and avoid confusion or gaslighting.

When faced with pushback like "You're overreacting," "I forgot," or "That's just how I am," don't feel you must endlessly explain yourself. Respond instead with: "I'm responsible for communicating my needs, and you're responsible for your response." Or say: "Whether intentional or not, the impact is the same for me." You don't have to justify or manage others' discomfort about your boundaries.

Boundary Escalation Log

Try this exercise: Create a chart with four columns:
Date - Boundary Set/Restated - Their Response - Next Step/Action Taken.

Use this log every time you feel uncertain or need guidance. Record your observations to spot patterns and reinforce your right to set boundaries. Afterward, review your entries to identify action steps. Next, let's discuss exactly how to rebuild trust when boundaries are crossed by you or someone else.

Repairing Trust After a Boundary Slip (Yours or Theirs)

Everyone slips up with boundaries sometimes, even confident people. You might loosen your limits to keep the peace, avoid awkwardness, or notice only later. Sometimes, someone you care about crosses a line by accident or out of habit. Setting boundaries takes practice, not perfection. Mistakes don't mean you're bad at boundaries; they mean you're human and learning. Repairing trust after a slip isn't about blame; it helps relationships, including the one you have with yourself, grow.

If you notice you let your boundary slip, or you crossed someone else's, the first thing to do is admit it. You can say something simple, like, "I realize I didn't stick to my boundary about work emails last night," or "I see that I pushed too hard about that topic when you asked me not to." Just naming what happened, without getting defensive, is powerful. Try not to downplay or explain it away. You don't need a long story or to go over every detail. A clear, direct admission eases tension and shows you're taking responsibility.

Next, offer a simple apology without excuses or blame for the other person. You might say, "I'm sorry I didn't stand by what I said," or "I apologize for stepping over your limit. That wasn't fair to you." This isn't about feeling ashamed or begging for forgiveness. It's about building trust by owning what you did. When we admit our mistakes honestly, we show others it's safe to be open and that problems can be fixed.

After you've admitted the slip and apologized, focus on what you'll do differently next time. This is how real repair starts, by turning intentions into actions. Say your plan out loud: "Next time, I'll speak up right away if I feel pressured," or "From now on, I'll pause before responding so I don't overcommit." Don't wait, choose one specific change now and make a commitment to yourself or someone else. You don't have to be perfect, but sharing your plan shows you mean it.

Forgiving yourself can be the hardest part, especially if you're used to being tough on yourself. When you start to feel ashamed, or your inner critic brings up old mistakes, remind yourself: "Every slip is a chance to learn and try again." This isn't just a nice saying; it's true. Setting boundaries is about making progress, not being perfect. If you start blaming yourself, say out loud or write: "I forgive myself for struggling; it means I'm growing." Growth is never perfect; it's often messy and awkward.

Different scenarios call for different scripts. If you need to apologize to a partner, be honest but gentle: "I promised to back off when you needed alone time, but I pushed anyway. I'm sorry, I want to do better." With a friend: "I realize I bailed on our plan after saying I'd prioritize our friendship. That wasn't fair to you." In the workplace: "I agreed to take on extra work despite setting a boundary about my capacity. I need to be more upfront next time." When someone comes to you with an apology for crossing your line, try responding with kindness: "Thank you for being honest. Let's figure out how to avoid this next time," or "I appreciate your apology, and I'd like to talk about what we need moving forward." If you're the one who slipped, but still want to keep working on this boundary, say: "I slipped, but I'm not giving up on this boundary."

Repairing trust isn't just about fixing one mistake. It's about creating a relationship where both people feel safe to be themselves, even if they're imperfect. Each time you repair, see it as a step forward, not a setback.

When to Walk Away, Recognizing When It's Time to Let Go

After you've tried to set clear boundaries and had the same talks over and over, you may need to ask yourself some tough questions. If someone keeps crossing your limits, ignores your needs, or makes you doubt yourself, it's time to think about whether this relationship is safe or healthy for you. This isn't about leaving at the first sign of trouble, but about protecting yourself when the other person won't respect you. If the cycle of hurt and repair never ends, apologies are empty or missing, and you feel worse every time you interact, the problem goes deeper. These patterns can show up in any relationship, romantic, friendship, work, or family.

Look out for warning signs. Emotional abuse is often quiet, not obvious. Repeated gaslighting (making you doubt your feelings or memories), threats like "no one else will want you," or ignoring your clear boundaries are all red flags. If you dread seeing someone, feel anxious before talking to them, or change your life to avoid their reactions, notice those feelings. Constant fear, feeling like you're walking on eggshells, or thinking you'll never be enough aren't just rough times; they're signs your safety or mental health could be at risk.

Check in with yourself: Do you mostly feel fear or anxiety around this person? Have you stopped speaking up because it's "not worth the fallout"? Are you always drained after being with them? Are you hiding your true self or lying to others to keep the peace? If you're consistently sacrificing your own well-being and there's no hope for change, it may be time to step away.

Leaving is hard. You might feel guilty or sad about ending a long friendship, quitting a job you cared about, or leaving a relationship that used to be loving. Relief and fear often come together; you're free from pain, but unsure about what's next. It's normal to doubt your strength or worry about being alone. Many people who left friendships, jobs, or marriages for these reasons felt guilty and afraid, but later found they had more room for themselves.

If you're considering leaving, make a plan. Don't disappear unless safety demands it. Decide what you need to say, keep it simple and direct: "I need to step back from this relationship to care for myself," or "This dynamic isn't working for me, so I'm moving on." Sometimes, "I wish you well, but I can't continue" is enough. Speak your truth: you don't owe an attack or defense; just honesty and clarity. If direct conversation feels unsafe or too hard, a written message works.

After you leave, there's often a quiet period as you start to heal. This is a good time to reach out to people who support you. Friends who respect your boundaries can check in with you. If you need it, therapy can help you work through grief and rebuild trust in yourself. Take care of your basic needs: eat, move your body, and rest, even if it's hard. Simple rituals, like writing a goodbye letter, deleting old messages, or clearing reminders when you're ready, can also help.

Self-Care After Ending a Relationship

- Keep their contact info only for emergencies; mute or block if necessary.

- Journal each night about your feelings for a week.

- Meet at least one trusted friend for support.

- Try guided meditations on letting go.

- Note three ways you protected yourself today.

- Join an online support group or forum for shared experiences.

Healing takes time. It's about making room for a future where your needs matter. Allow yourself to move forward and build new, healthier chapters in your life.

"My Situation Is Different" Troubleshooting Complex or Unique Scenarios

If you've ever read advice about boundaries and thought, "My life is more complicated than that," you're not alone. Maybe you live with someone who ignores your limits, co-parent with a difficult ex, depend on your job for money, or care for someone else. Cultural expectations and family history can also make setting boundaries much harder than most advice suggests. It can feel lonely or even embarrassing to struggle when boundaries seem easier for others to set.

Your situation is serious, and boundaries should fit your reality. They look different in tight living spaces, shared custody, multigenerational homes, or when money limits your choices. If you can't just leave a job, move out, or cut ties, you need tools that work for your life.

If speaking up directly could make things worse, being subtle can help. If you're worried about backlash or things getting worse, put your safety first. Use small boundaries, like saying, "I can't talk about that topic right now," or "Let's keep it to logistics." These protect your energy and help keep things calm. In tough living situations, routines like wearing earbuds, locking your door for breaks, or only talking about what's necessary can give you mental space. Even small, steady boundaries can make a big difference.

If you're financially dependent on someone or can't risk losing your job, try the "minimum effective dose": set the smallest boundary that still helps you. If work culture pushes you to socialize after hours, but it drains you, politely skip it sometimes and gradually do it more often. If your boss wants instant replies to texts after work, answer the next morning with a quick, "Just saw this, will handle today." Even without a big announcement, people start to notice and respect your new patterns.

Co-parenting with a difficult ex can be especially tough. You might have to talk for your kids' sake, even if your ex tries to manipulate you. Keep it businesslike: "Let's stick to the schedule," or "I'll reply to messages about the kids." Be brief and clear, and don't let them draw you into arguments. If things get out of hand or feel unsafe, write everything down and think about getting legal or mediation help to protect yourself and your children.

Having support is important. Who can help you? Maybe a trusted friend who checks in, a therapist to help you plan, or a peer group that understands your situation. If you keep having boundary problems at work, talk to HR, keep records, and ask about company policies. In families or caregiving roles where power is uneven, reach out to advocacy groups or online communities. Many people find strength in cultural groups where others understand the balance between tradition and self-care.

Troubleshooting Decision Tree

- If direct conversation feels unsafe → Use micro-boundaries; keep it practical.

- If financial dependence is a barrier → Set subtle boundaries; find small ways to claim time and space.

- If ongoing contact is required (co-parenting/caregiving) → Stick to logistics, keep talk brief, seek outside support.

- If power dynamics are complex → Document everything, and

reach out to legal/HR or advocacy resources.

Messy situations need creative solutions and flexibility. Celebrate small victories, a quiet evening, a conversation without drama, or a moment you took back for yourself. Adjusting to your situation shows real strength.

As we wrap up, remember that every boundary matters, even the small ones, especially when life is complicated. You don't need to be perfect; keep making progress that works for you. The next chapter will share ways to keep your boundaries strong and flexible as your life changes, because boundaries grow and change with you.

Chapter Ten

Maintenance, Growth, and Life Transitions

The 30-Day "Boundary Bootcamp" Action Plan for Habit-Building

Have you ever meant to stop scrolling through your phone but lost track of time? Our brains favor routines, even unhelpful ones. Scripts aren't useful when tired or caught off guard, and old people-pleasing habits can resurface. That's why I created a 30-day "Boundary Bootcamp," a step-by-step plan to make boundary-setting automatic, with steady progress through small wins that boost your confidence and resilience.

Setting boundaries is like building a muscle; the more you practice, even in small ways, the stronger it gets. Don't wait for a crisis. This plan starts with personal limits, then expands to acquaintances, friends, family, work, and groups. If life gets hectic or stressful, feel free to adjust the daily challenges or take extra time on certain steps. This flexibility helps you stay committed and ensures your boundary-setting remains relevant to your current situation.

Here's a sample overview of the month, showing how each day's challenge builds on the previous day, creating a clear, step-by-step progression through different focus areas.

- Days 1-4 begin with setting personal limits:

  - Day 1, choose a small personal rule like no email after 8 pm or taking quiet time before bed.

  - Day 2, practice delaying your response by saying, "I'll check my calendar and get back to you."

  - Days 3 and 4, continue practicing these habits.

- Days 5-7: add pauses before responding and protect your time by waiting 5 minutes before saying yes or keeping your lunch break free.

- Days 8-10 expand boundaries to low-risk interactions: practice a gentle "no" with someone, such as a store clerk.

- Days 11-14 move to rewriting internal beliefs, such as changing "I should always help" to "I can support without abandoning myself."

- Days 15-20 introduce boundaries in social and work settings: use scripts in group chats, notice personal energy drains, and set limits with friends or at work. Each set of days continues from the last, so by the time you reach later challenges, you are using skills built earlier, reinforcing growth and confidence as you move from simple to more complex situations.

As the month ends, use these daily prompts:

- Days 21–24, deepen your practice, stand firm if someone pushes back, repeat your "no" without apologizing, and send reminders about your limits, like updating your status or using an out-of-office reply.

- Day 25: Reflect in your journal about a recent win, notice your feelings, and track any physical changes. This cements growth and builds self-trust.

- Days 26–29: focus on boundaries when tired or triggered, rest rather than overcommit, set a needed limit on someone challenging, or ask for support.

- Day 30: Celebrate using your habit tracker and reflect on your journey. Recognize your efforts, no matter how small, and acknowledge your growth. Celebrating these wins reinforces your new habits and boosts your confidence, making it easier to maintain boundaries beyond the 30 days.

Tracking matters because it shows your progress. There's a printable or digital tracker (see below). Note the date, action, even "noticed urge but didn't act," your feelings, and surprises. Over time, you'll spot patterns, maybe Mondays are tougher, or saying no may get easier with certain people. The tracker isn't just for accountability; it proves your resilience when you doubt yourself.

Your Boundary Bootcamp Log

- **Date - Daily Action - Mood - Notes/Reflections**

- Day 1 - No email after 8 pm. - Calm. - Slept better; felt less tense.

- Day 2 - Paused before saying yes. - Anxious/Relief - Hard at first, then empowering.

- ....

- Day 25 - Journaled about recent win. - Happy - Proudly realized I stood up for myself.

Motivation needs regular boosts. Each day, say an affirmation like: "I protect my peace today," "My boundaries deserve respect," "My needs are not a burden," or "Each small step counts." You can say them out loud or write them in your phone. Accountability helps, too: text a friend about a milestone ("I finally said no at work!") or share your wins in an online group. If you don't like making changes alone, find a "boundary buddy" to talk through setbacks and celebrate progress together.

You don't have to be perfect; keep showing up for yourself in small, honest ways. Every little boundary you set creates more calm and self-respect. In 30 days, these small steps can lead to changes and confidence that last long after any workshop or conversation.

Quarterly Boundary Check-Ins, Keeping Your Progress on Track

Boundaries can slip, even when you think you've mastered them. One month, you're on track; next, you're saying yes to draining things or slipping into old habits. It's part of life, not failure. Regular check-ins make a difference. Taking time every few months to pause, reflect, and adjust boundaries is real self-care. It's not about criticizing mistakes or aiming for perfection. It's about recognizing the need for change in roles and relationships. Give yourself the same care you'd give to anything that's growing, like a plant, a friendship, or favorite projects. These check-ins help you grow, not judge yourself.

A quarterly review isn't just for when things go wrong; it's a regular part of life. Treat it as a seasonal checkup for your mental health. Instead of waiting for problems to arise, you catch small issues early. This is when you notice boundary drift, like replying to late-night work emails or always answering calls from a friend who vents. Pausing to ask, "Where am I slipping?" helps you spot areas needing attention. It's also a chance to see what's working: maybe you protect weekends better, or your family gives you notice before visits. Wins and slips both matter and deserve attention.

To make this process easier, try using a Quarterly Boundary Review worksheet with prompts and checklists to keep things focused but flexible. Start by asking yourself: "Which boundaries have stuck? Where do I feel drained or resentful? What feels easier than before?" Then get specific: "What new challenges have come up? Are there people or situations where I'm struggling more?" Don't just look at problems, notice where you've made progress, where scripts have worked, or where a limit that once felt hard now feels natural. Use a checklist for different parts of your life: work, family, friendships, romance, and self-care. Rate each one: Are my limits clear here? Do I feel safe and respected? Am I slipping into old habits with anyone? This kind of reflection helps you spot issues before they get out of hand.

The review also helps you set intentions for what's next. Once you notice patterns, ask yourself: "Which boundaries need to be stronger? Is there a conversation I'm avoiding? Should I change a script?" Maybe a coworker pushes your limits, or a family member tries to make you feel guilty when you say no. Plan how to reset, whether that's having a direct talk, writing a note, or just repeating your limit more clearly. If your scripts feel awkward, rewrite them in your own words.

Don't let guilt get in the way. Boundaries change as your life changes. If you slip up or let a boundary slide, it's not a disaster. Instead of being hard on yourself, see it as useful information. Ask yourself: "What got in my way? What support do I need this time?" Sometimes just saying the challenge out loud makes it feel less overwhelming.

To make these check-ins last, add them to your calendar. Starting each season works well for many women. Treat it like a quarterly date with yourself. Pair it with something you enjoy so it doesn't feel like a chore: maybe a solo coffee at your favorite café, an afternoon with music and a new journal, or ordering takeout from a place you love but rarely visit. Rituals matter because they turn maintenance into celebration, not just another task.

Digital reminders can help you keep this ritual going when life gets busy. Set a recurring calendar event, an alert on your phone, or put a sticky note in your planner as a prompt. If you like visuals, make a playlist of songs that remind you of strength or peace and listen while you reflect. If you're motivated by treats, plan a reward after each review: buy a scented candle, schedule a massage, or take an hour for something you enjoy.

The point of these check-ins isn't to be perfect, but to notice your progress and stay present. Each review is a chance to see how far you've come, gently reset where needed, and recommit to the boundaries that keep you at peace. Use this time to update your scripts, fix any slips without shame, and set new goals for the next few months. The more you make this a habit, the easier it is to see what's working and what needs attention, before burnout or resentment builds up. This is about self-respect, not pressure; it's how you keep showing up for yourself, no matter what life brings.

Adapting Boundaries for Life Changes, New Jobs, Motherhood, Moving, and More

Life is always changing. One day you're at your old job, and the next you're starting something new, moving to a new city, becoming a parent, ending a relationship, or facing changes in your health. Each change affects more than just your schedule; it changes your relationships and what you need from others. When life shifts, your boundaries need to adjust, too. Sometimes they need to be looser, sometimes tighter. It's normal to check in and realign them from time to time.

Big changes often show you where old boundaries don't fit anymore. For example, a new job brings new expectations and coworkers. You might need to make it clear that you won't answer emails after hours, even if your last job expected it. Early on, people notice your boundaries, and if you don't set them, others might set them for you. If a supervisor expects you to reply to Slack messages after dinner, you can say, "I'm excited to join the team, and I sign off at 7 pm to recharge." Being assertive helps avoid misunderstandings, and setting limits isn't rude; it's necessary.

Becoming a parent is another big change. Your energy gets pulled in ways you didn't expect, and loved ones might want to help more than you want, or need more attention than you can give. Don't be afraid to say, "We're keeping visits short while we settle in as new parents," or let friends know that evenings are now for family. Protecting what feels healthy, even if it disappoints others, is important.

Moving to a new place means finding a balance between wanting connection and needing space. Being far from your old support network, you might feel pressure to stay in close contact while you build new routines. It's okay to tell friends, "Let's schedule calls while I adapt to my new routine," so they know you're not rejecting them if you talk less. If you're going back to school, your calendar can fill up fast. Let people know, "I need my weeknights for studying, so I'll be less available," to help them respect your priorities.

After a relationship ends, boundaries matter even more. Friends might take sides or want details, and family may offer advice or push you to move on. In these times, clear boundaries help protect you: "I'm not ready to talk about it," or "I need some space before dating again," can give you the space you need.

Health changes, such as a diagnosis, injury, or chronic illness, also mean you need to reset your expectations. You might not be able to do everything you used to. Let others know, "I'm focusing on my health and need more rest." Even if people expect your usual responses, now is the time to put your needs first.

To make changing boundaries easier, try a transition boundary audit. Ask yourself: What's different now? Who needs to know about my new boundaries? Where am I struggling most? Whose expectations might not match mine? Look at the areas of your life that feel unsettled: work, family, social obligations, caregiving, and note what feels manageable. Decide which boundaries need to change right away and which can wait.

Once you've mapped things out, your next step is to communicate. Use simple scripts that fit your situation. For a job: "I'm available during office hours but not in the evenings." As a new parent: "Visits are welcome but need to be brief so we can rest." After a move: "I'm still getting settled. Can we schedule weekend calls?" If you're back in school: "Weeknights are for studying."

People may push back because changes can unsettle those used to your old ways. If someone says, "But you always..." or "This isn't like before," you can reply, "I know it's different, but here's what I need now." If you feel guilty or things get awkward, offer some flexibility without giving up your needs: "Let's try this for a few weeks, then check in." This shows you're open, but still keeping your limits.

Transitions can also bring feelings of loneliness or uncertainty. Finding support, such as a parenting group, professional network, student circle, or illness support group, can be really helpful as you adjust your boundaries. Others in similar situations can offer practical advice and emotional support.

In the end, every big change is a chance to update your boundaries. Even if it feels uncomfortable or others resist, you deserve limits that fit your life as it is now. Share your needs early and kindly, keep your boundaries steady when challenged, and give yourself room to adjust as things settle into a new normal.

Celebrating Small Wins, Building Confidence Through Micro-Success

Setting boundaries isn't always dramatic. It often happens in small, everyday choices, like telling your roommate you'll do the dishes later or saying no to a last-minute meeting. These moments might seem minor, but they're key to real change. If you wait to feel accomplished until your boundaries are perfect, you'll miss out on the satisfaction of progress. Real confidence and self-trust come from noticing these small wins—the little changes that add up over time.

Celebrating small wins is backed by science; our brains love positive reinforcement. Every time you notice and celebrate a boundary success, your brain releases dopamine, which helps the new habit stick. This reward is key to building new patterns. If you ignore your progress, self-doubt can grow, and setbacks feel worse. By appreciating your wins, you teach yourself that you're capable and deserve respect, from yourself and others.

You don't need big gestures to celebrate. Sometimes it's just a private moment. You might write a note in your journal about standing your ground, add a sticker to your tracker for every "no" you say, or do a quick dance in your kitchen after a tough moment. Even looking in the mirror and saying, "That was hard, but I did it," can be powerful. These personal rituals aren't silly; they remind you that every step matters.

Sometimes, sharing your progress with someone else makes your achievements feel even bigger. You might text a friend, "Guess what? I said no to extra work today!" or share your story in a group chat or online. If you have a boundary buddy, celebrate each other's wins. Whether you share publicly or privately, this acknowledgment makes your success feel real, builds accountability, and reminds you that progress matters.

To help you reflect and celebrate, try using simple prompts after a boundary win, like, "Today I said no and felt..." or "I stood up for myself and noticed..." Don't just focus on wins that went perfectly, even if you felt awkward or guilty; recognizing your effort helps you grow. Over time, these notes show your journey and remind you how far you've come.

Try keeping a "Boundary Wins" log. Set up a notebook or digital page with columns for the date, situation, script you used, outcome, and your feelings. For example:

- **Date - Situation - Script Used - Outcome - Feelings**

- 4/2 - Declined weekend work - "I need this weekend for myself." - The boss accepted. - Nervous, but proud

- 4/14 - Limited friend venting - "I have ten minutes to chat." -

Friend agreed. - Relieved.

- 4/22 - Set family visit time - "Let's keep it to two hours." - Family surprised. - calm

Looking over this log every few months gives you real proof of your growth, even if you feel stuck. If you like visuals, make a vision board with clippings, photos, or words that show your boundary wins, moments of peace, strength, or freedom you've created by setting limits. You might include an open window for breathing room, or the word "No" in bold.

Reviewing your log or vision board isn't just about patting yourself on the back; it's about seeing proof that you can do this. When setbacks happen (and they will), looking back at your small wins can keep you motivated. You'll remember you've handled tough situations before and can do it again.

Reflection is important. Ask yourself: What did this win mean to me? Did I feel lighter, less resentful, or sleep better? These aren't small changes; they show real personal growth. Every small success reminds you that your needs matter.

Over time, this practice does more than boost your confidence; it changes how you see yourself. Boundaries stop feeling like awkward experiments and become part of who you are, bringing relief and pride.

Small wins are the building blocks of lasting change. By noticing, honoring, and celebrating them, on your own or with others, you keep motivation alive during hard times. As you keep stacking up these successes, remind yourself: every step counts, every limit is important, and all progress is worth recognition. Up next, we'll explore tools and resources to help you sustain these habits and make your boundaries work.

Chapter Eleven

Tools And Resources for Everyday Empowerment

The Ultimate Boundary Script Bank, Fill-in-the-Blank Phrases for Every Scenario

Everyone has been there: staring at your phone for the right response that's honest but won't start family drama, or feeling caught off guard at work when someone tests your limits. Boundary scripts serve as tools to empower you, providing language that feels true to you, whether you want to be gentle, direct, or firm, helping you maintain your well-being under stress or guilt.

There isn't one phrase for every situation, so it helps to have options. Sometimes, you can say, "I appreciate you thinking of me, but I'll pass this time." Other times, "I'm not able to do that" is best. If someone pushes, use, "I've made my decision, and I'm not open to discussing it further." Scripts are flexible, letting you choose what fits the moment and your style. In the following section, you'll find options for different relationships and situations, so you're prepared for tough moments. Let's explore how to tailor scripts for different relationships to help you feel more confident in your boundaries.

Boundary Scripts by Category:

To help you quickly find the right language, the scripts below are organized by relationship type, so you can feel more secure and respected when setting boundaries.

Family Boundaries: Family boundaries can get blurry. You can start gently by saying, "I need a heads-up before we make plans." If a cousin keeps showing up without warning, try, "I need advance notice before visits, please call or text first." For family members who keep pushing, you might say, "I realize this is new, but my boundary isn't changing." If your family communicates more indirectly, you can personalize your approach: "Out of respect for our traditions, I want to share what matters to me and why." In group settings, try inclusive phrases like, "Let's figure out a plan that supports everyone, including me." To make boundaries clearer, adapt these scripts to your specific family dynamics and communication style.

Work Boundaries: Scripts tailored for the workplace can help maintain professionalism. Being assertive at work can sometimes be mistaken for being rude, especially for women. If you have too much on your plate, you can say, "Given my current workload, I can't take on another project." If the pressure keeps coming, try, "Given my workload, I can't cover that, but I can help prioritize." For people who keep asking, say, "I'm not available for extra work outside my role." Stick to the facts: "I'm at capacity and can't meet that deadline." For digital boundaries, you might use, "So that you know, I'm offline after 6 p.m.; I'll respond tomorrow."

Friend Boundaries: Scripts for friendships can help you balance care with self-respect. With friends, setting boundaries can feel tough because you don't want to let anyone down. A gentle no: "Thanks for thinking of me, but I'm not available for dinner tonight." If a friend persists: "I need some solo time tonight; let's reconnect later this week." For guilt: "I care about you, but my answer hasn't changed." For ongoing issues: "I'm prioritizing my well-being and need to step back from plans for now." Boundaries can feel especially tricky in romantic relationships, and deserve their own attention.

Romantic Relationship Boundaries: Scripts for Intimate Partners Address Unique Challenges. Expressing needs gently: "I care about you and need some time alone."

- Dividing chores: "I need us to talk about how we split tasks so things feel balanced."
- Navigating intimacy: "I want us both comfortable, so let's slow down."
- Managing digital space: "To protect my peace, I turn off my phone after 9 p.m. If it's important, we can talk tomorrow."

Online/Digital Life: Online life brings its own challenges, requiring clear digital boundaries. Here are some scripts for common online situations, organized by category. For group chat boundaries, you can say, "Just FYI, I mute notifications after 8 p.m. to unwind." When responding to persistent messages, use, "I already answered; my decision stands." To set limits ahead of time, say, "I'm not available for late-night texts; let's talk during the day." For uncomfortable topics, opt for, "I'd rather not discuss that here; let's keep things positive." With digital boundaries set, it's important to be prepared for situations where others may not respect them.

Pushback/Boundary Violations: Scripts can also help when someone pushes back or crosses your boundaries. If someone tries to guilt-trip you, say, "I know this is hard, but my boundary isn't changing." If they say they forgot, respond with, "Even if you forgot, I need this respected from now on." For manipulation, you can say, "It's important I'm honest about what I can and can't do, even if that's disappointing." Once you get comfortable with scripts, you can develop your personal style for every relationship.

Finding Your Go-To Script Style

Spend five minutes listing situations where setting boundaries feels hardest, maybe with your parents, your boss, or a close friend. Choose one scenario and try all three script styles: gentle, firm, and strong. Notice which one feels natural. Practicing these will help you trust your ability to handle boundary conversations confidently and reduce anxiety over time. Rewrite each script in your own words and keep your favorites where you can see them when needed.

Boundary scripts aren't magic, but they are powerful tools for having honest, confident conversations. Practice using them to turn nervous energy into action, protect your peace, and build real connections. To help put these scripts into practice, let's explore tools and worksheets to support your boundary-setting journey.

Worksheets and Checklists, Roadmaps for Real Life

Writing your thoughts down can be a big relief, especially when working on boundaries. When stuck in "should I or shouldn't I?" decisions, worksheets and checklists break things into steps. That's why I've made printable tools to use when you feel stuck or uncertain, or when you want to track progress. These are designed to guide you through the confusion and self-doubt that come with setting boundaries.

Start with the "Boundary Barometer" quiz (Chapter 2). It quickly checks how you handle boundaries at work, with family, friends, and yourself. Rate your reactions, record your answers, and reflect on your strengths and areas needing improvement. Some areas may be strong; others may need attention.

Next, use the "Top Values" list (Chapter 2) to focus on your core values. List values like honesty or independence and connect each to a boundary you want to protect. Setting boundaries is easier when you know what drives them.

It's not always easy to notice your triggers. That's why the "Trigger Tracker" helps. Jot down unsettling interactions, who was involved, what was said, and how you felt. Over time, you'll see patterns and know what or who usually throws you off, making surprises less likely.

Checklists help you keep up progress. Use a daily or weekly boundary checklist to notice if you're slipping into old habits, without expecting perfection. Ask: Did I say yes when I wanted to say no? Did I make time for myself? Was I drained after a certain interaction? These check-ins help you spot problems early.

Before a tough conversation, use a prep checklist. Write down who you'll talk to, your goal, when and where you'll meet, and how you want to show up. Plan what you'll do if things get tense, like pausing or taking a breath. After the conversation, check in with yourself: Did you notice your feelings and take care of yourself, maybe with a walk or snack? Remember, self-care is part of the process.

Fill-in-the-blank templates make planning boundary conversations less intimidating. The conversation planner helps lay out who's involved, what you want to say, how to start, and possible challenges. There's also space for backup phrases if you get nervous. Afterward, use a reflection worksheet to note what went well and what you'd do differently. Each attempt helps you grow.

To stay motivated, try the 30-day "Boundary Bootcamp" (Chapter 10). It's a visual way to see your daily progress, mark each day you pause before saying yes, or use a new script. Use the "Boundary Wins" log (Chapter 10) to celebrate every victory. Each win is proof of progress.

Set check-ins with yourself every few months, using a review template to reflect on what's working, what needs to change, and what support you need. Ask: What am I proud of? Where am I having trouble? Looking back, you'll see your progress.

With these tools, you don't have to set boundaries alone or wonder about your progress. Every worksheet, checklist, and tracker helps you build stronger boundaries and shows you, step by step, that you're moving forward. When resistance arises, decision trees can offer structured guidance on what to do next.

Decision Trees for Resistance To Assist In What to Do When They Push Back

If you've had someone ignore your boundaries, push back, or try to guilt you, you know how quickly things can escalate. Saying what you need is one thing, but holding firm when someone resists is another. That's where decision trees help. Think of them as a mental map guiding you through every "what now?" moment, so you don't freeze, second-guess yourself, or give in from exhaustion. The first step: Did they respect your boundary? If yes, breathe and celebrate. If not, the tree shows you what to do next.

When someone pushes back, the kind of resistance matters. Let's start with guilt-tripping. If you feel responsible for their emotions, like when you hear "If you cared, you'd help...", pause and check in with yourself. Ask whose discomfort this really is, and if it's yours to carry. Remember, having empathy doesn't mean you have to ignore your own needs. If you want to give in to keep the peace, use your decision tree: if saying "no" makes you feel guilty, kindly but firmly restate your need. If the guilt turns into emotional blackmail, move to the next step, limit the conversation, or step away if things get heated.

Manipulation can look different. Maybe someone says they "forgot" your boundary or tries to downplay your request by saying, "You're being dramatic." When this happens, don't get pulled into arguing the facts. Give a clear reminder: "Even if you forgot, my expectation hasn't changed." Say it once, then move on. Denial can be even harder; if they refuse to acknowledge what you've said, don't get stuck explaining yourself over and over. Keep it simple: name what's happening, restate your position, and avoid over-explaining.

When things start to escalate, like raised voices, anger, or passive-aggressive comments, the decision tree branches again. Your main goal is to protect your sense of safety and control. If someone yells or tries to intimidate you, pause or step away. Sometimes, leaving is the only way to calm things down. If you can't leave, like in a work meeting or family dinner, use short statements such as, "I'm not comfortable with this conversation right now," and come back to it later when things are calmer.

Repeated requests can be tough. You've said no two or three times, but the person keeps asking. This is when your decision tree tells you to reinforce your boundary, then take action. Restate what you can and can't do, and if it happens again, explain the consequence or limit contact for a while. For example, if a coworker keeps giving you extra work even after you've set limits, let them know you'll involve your supervisor if it continues.

Sometimes, resistance goes from uncomfortable to unsafe. If you ever feel threatened, emotionally or physically, the decision tree stops here: leave and get support right away. Your safety comes first. Reach out to someone you trust or get professional help. It takes strength to know when a situation is bigger than one conversation.

Keeping track of stubborn resistance isn't just for legal or HR reasons; it's also a way to protect yourself. Write down each time someone pushes back: when it happened, what was said, and how you responded. This helps you spot patterns and avoid doubting yourself. Having a record gives you confidence if you need to talk to a supervisor, therapist, mediator, or even get legal help. If repeated resistance starts to affect your mental health or daily life, don't hesitate to reach out for extra support.

Decision trees aren't about reacting like a robot; they're about finding clarity when emotions are high and things feel confusing. Each branch is a lifeline. Whether resistance is subtle or intense, you'll have a way forward. Practice your responses ahead of time, picture the tree during tough moments, and remember that every step you take to enforce your boundaries is a win, even if it means walking away from people who won't respect them.

Resource Roundup, Podcasts, Apps, Communities, and Further Reading

Support doesn't stop when you finish this book. You don't have to figure things out alone, and sometimes the best help comes from hearing someone else's story, a real conversation, or a practical tip. Podcasts are easy to fit into your day, whether you're commuting, cleaning, or walking. "We Can Do Hard Things," with Glennon Doyle, is a favorite among many women because it feels like chatting with friends who are honest about life's messiness and growth. Another great option is "Therapy for Black Girls," which offers personal, practical guidance on mental health and relationships for women of color. For quick, helpful advice, check out Nedra Glover Tawwab's Instagram; her posts get right to the point about boundaries and self-worth. If you like audiobooks or YouTube, look for playlists and interviews with experts on topics like assertiveness or healing after toxic relationships. Search for channels with real-life stories or Q&A sessions. Sometimes, hearing about someone else's journey makes your own challenges feel less lonely.

Every day life can feel overwhelming, and it's easy to fall back into old habits without reminders. That's where digital tools help. Headspace offers short guided meditations and mindfulness exercises that can quickly reset your mood. If you want to check in with yourself, Day One is a simple journaling app for tracking feelings, wins, and struggles. To build better habits around self-care or saying "no," Habitica and Streaks make tracking your progress visual and rewarding. These apps help make boundary-setting a regular part of your life, not just something you do in a crisis. If you like paper, using a habit tracker alongside phone reminders works too.

Not everyone has a supportive group of friends or family who understands. That's why online spaces matter. The #BoundariesAreBeautiful hashtag on Instagram and Twitter connects you with women sharing their own wins and scripts. Sometimes, you'll find the perfect phrase for your next conversation. Reddit has helpful communities like r/relationships and r/selfimprovement, where you can ask questions and get advice from people who've been through it. Many women's support groups and book clubs now meet online; these are safe places to share resources, talk about tough days, or just be heard by others working on the same skills. Encouragement from peers makes it easier to try new scripts or stick to your boundaries when things get tough.

If you want to dive deeper, some books have shaped how women think about boundaries for years. "Set Boundaries, Find Peace" by Nedra Glover Tawwab is a practical guide with real examples and step-by-step advice for all kinds of relationships. Harriet Lerner's "The Dance of Anger" explores the emotional patterns that keep women stuck in people-pleasing or silence, and shows how to break that cycle without causing chaos. "Codependent No More" by Melody Beattie is a classic for anyone who's lost themselves while caring for others or felt guilty about saying no. Workbooks based on these books often include exercises, prompts, and honest discussions about how culture, upbringing, and personality shape your boundaries.

You don't have to do this alone or start from scratch. If you like learning by listening, search for interviews with boundary experts on Spotify or Apple Podcasts. Hearing new perspectives can give you courage on tough days. Sometimes, joining a supportive WhatsApp group or Facebook community is all you need to see that you're not alone. Each resource offers something unique, practical tips, empathy, real-life stories, motivation, or just a reminder that growth happens one step at a time.

Chapter Twelve

Glossary, Modern Slang, Lingo, and Terms Every Boundary-Setter Should Know

Language is powerful, especially when it comes to boundaries. Knowing the right words helps you spot patterns, talk about tough issues, and notice red flags early. Here's a simple glossary of common terms so you can use them confidently with friends, coworkers, or for your own reflection.

People-pleasing happens when you feel you must always prioritize others' needs over your own, constantly saying yes to favors even when overwhelmed. It's more than just being nice; it's a habit that eventually drains you. Emotional labor refers to the invisible work of managing emotions, yours and everyone else's. At home, that could mean easing conflict or remembering birthdays; at work, it might be keeping morale up when you yourself need support. This often-unseen work is tiring.

Gaslighting is a manipulative tactic that makes you question your reality, like when someone denies clear facts ("You're too sensitive, that never happened"), undermining your confidence over time. Enmeshment describes a lack of clear boundaries, often in families, where emotional lines blur so much that it's hard to separate oneself from others.

Ghosting, popularized in online dating, refers to abruptly cutting off communication, leaving the other person without closure. This can trigger confusion and self-doubt. A red flag signals a warning that something's off in a relationship; for example, someone who disregards your boundaries or always centers themselves.

Boundary pushback happens when people resist your limits by guilt-tripping, ignoring, or repeatedly asking after you've said no. Though uncomfortable, it's normal. An energy vampire is someone who exhausts you emotionally, often by complaining, demanding attention, or ignoring your needs.

Codependency is when you're so focused on someone else's needs that you lose sight of your own. In Western contexts, this is considered unhealthy; in some cultures, close support is normal, so context matters. A behavior labeled codependent in one setting may be considered typical support in another.

Emotional regulation is the skill of recognizing and managing strong feelings before they take over. Self-reminders like "I'm allowed to say no" help keep your reaction in check. Love bombing occurs when someone overwhelms you with excessive affection or gifts early in a relationship, typically to control rather than genuinely care for you.

Passive-aggressive behavior is expressing anger indirectly, such as giving the silent treatment or making cutting remarks rather than addressing issues openly. Triangulation draws a third party into conflict to manipulate or pressure you ("Even your sister agrees with me"). Both are ways to avoid healthy boundaries.

You don't have to memorize these terms all at once. Try using them in your conversations and self-talk. For example, saying "I need to protect my energy" is a simple way to turn down plans without guilt, and "That's a red flag for me" lets you say something feels wrong. Naming what's happening helps you stay grounded and assertive.

Culture can affect how these words are understood. At home, "emotional labor" might just be called caring, while at work, it could mean unfair pressure. Words like "gaslighting" or "codependency" can mean different things in different communities, so check for confusion and use them carefully.

Learning these words gives you more tools for setting boundaries. You'll start to notice these patterns in yourself and others, and soon, these terms will feel natural. The more comfortable you get with this language, the easier it is to spot issues early and speak up for your needs.

Most importantly, language isn't just for describing problems; it helps you build solutions and healthier habits in your relationships. With these words, you'll be better able to spot issues early and express your needs, making hard conversations less scary and much more empowering.

This glossary is more than just a reference; it's a bridge to the life you want, where you feel supported, respected, and understood. Keep these words in mind as you build stronger habits and healthier relationships.

Conclusion

If you're reading these final words, take a moment to let that sink in. You made the effort for yourself. Instead of just wishing for better boundaries, you took action. You learned, reflected, practiced, and maybe stumbled along the way. That's real growth, messy, honest, and made up of small, brave steps. Recognizing your progress can fill you with pride and motivate you to continue your efforts.

When I started writing this, my goal was clear: I wanted women like you, especially those balancing work, relationships, family, and their own feelings, to feel seen and strong. This book isn't about shutting people out. It's about listening to yourself, claiming your space, and protecting your peace. You truly deserve this.

Take a moment to recognize what you've achieved. You can now spot red flags, manipulation, guilt-tripping, energy drains, and people-pleasing. You've identified your values and triggers, figured out what needs protecting, and practiced real scripts so you don't have to second-guess yourself. We talked about family drama, friendship issues, work burnout, romantic confusion, and everyday situations where boundaries get blurry.

You've faced tough feelings like guilt, anxiety, and fear of rejection. These are real and can feel overwhelming. Now, you can tell the difference between your conscience guiding you and toxic guilt that holds you back. You've learned to steady yourself, stand firm when challenged, and keep your limits even when others push. And if you slip, you know how to forgive yourself and start again, because everyone needs grace.

Most importantly, you now know that boundaries aren't selfish; they're a form of self-respect. Setting a boundary doesn't take away from others; it creates space for real, honest connection. You have the right to protect your time, energy, feelings, and dreams. Every woman does, no matter her background or story.

This is more than just theory. You now have real tools: scripts for tough situations, checklists and worksheets to help you plan and reflect, and a 30-day Boundary Bootcamp with regular check-ins. You also have access to podcasts, apps, and communities. Remember, you're not alone in this journey, and community support can strengthen your confidence and resilience.

Remember, every effort you've made to honor your needs matters, no matter how small. If setbacks happen, use them as learning opportunities. Some days you'll feel strong, and other days old habits or pushback might throw you off. That's normal. Progress isn't always a straight line. It's okay to go back to scripts or ask for help. Celebrate every time you speak up or notice you want something different. That's how change begins.

Start today by using your boundary skills in real life. Don't wait for the perfect moment or a crisis. Begin with something small, like saying a gentle no to a friend, replying to a text later, or trying a new script with your family. The more you practice, the more natural it will feel.

Keep in mind that boundaries aren't the same for everyone. Your culture, family, and relationships shape what feels right for you. Use the tools in this book in ways that fit your life and respect your background. For example, consider cultural norms around communication or family roles. What matters most is that you feel safe, respected, and true to yourself. There's no prize for perfect boundaries, just you, learning and adjusting as you go.

As you move forward, remember you don't have to do this alone. Connect with others who are also learning to set boundaries. Use community resources, join a support group, or start your own support circle. Share your successes and struggles, and ask for advice. Sometimes, knowing you're not alone can help you keep going. You're not starting from scratch.

You're starting from experience, wisdom, and courage. You've already proven to yourself that you are worthy of care. You are allowed to change. You are allowed to take up space. And you are allowed to have relationships that feel good, not just "fine."

Setting boundaries isn't something you do just once. It's a lifelong practice, a conversation you keep having with yourself and others. Some days it will feel easy, and other days it will take all your courage. Keep revisiting your boundary scripts, reflect on your progress, and adjust as needed. That's okay. What matters is that you keep showing. Here's my final wish for you: Trust your heart, speak your truth, and always believe your needs are important. May your boundaries bring you peace and joy, and help your relationships lift you. Remember, even in tough times, you matter; your voice and your happiness matter. You are never alone on this journey.

Thank you for letting me share this journey with you. Now it's your turn to go out and claim the life and relationships you deserve. Others might benefit from this book, too, but they need your help. If you found it helpful, please leave an honest review so others can see its value. Thank you.

— George Munson

References

Aviv, E., Waizman, Y., Kim, E., Liu, J., Rodsky, E., & Saxbe, D. (2024). Cognitive household labor: gender disparities and consequences for maternal mental health and wellbeing. *Archives of Women S Mental Health, 28*(1), 5–14. https://doi.org/10.1007/s00737-024-01490-w

Boundaries test. (2026, February 10). Psychology Today. https://www.psychologytoday.com/us/tests/relationships/boundaries-test

Brenner, B., PhD. (2025). Squeezed in the middle: balancing act of the sandwich generation. *Therapy Group of DC.* https://therapygroupdc.com/therapist-dc-blog/squeezed-in-the-middle-balancing-act-of-the-sandwich-generation/

Byrne, E. K. (2020, May 13). *5 steps for women to combat Burnout.* Harvard Business Review. https://hbr.org/2020/05/5-steps-for-women-to-combat-burnout

Center, B. a. C. (2025, August 4). Top 10 manipulation tactics and how to Counter them | Bay Area CBT Center. *Bay Area CBT Center.* https://bayareacbtcenter.com/top-10-manipulation-tactics-and-how-to-counter-them/

Cowie, A. (2026, January 28). *Setting boundaries in a digital workplace — Producing Paradise.* Producing Paradise. https://www.producingparadise.com/self-improvement/setting-boundaries-in-a-digital-workplace/

DeVon, C. (2024, November 10). *How to say "no" when family and friends ask to borrow money, from a financial therapist*. CNBC. https://www.cnbc.com/2024/11/10/how-to-say-no-when-family-and-friends-ask-to-borrow-money.html

Elkington, H. (2024, March 4). [unlocked] The 30 day boundary setting challenge! Let's go. *In The Making*. https://www.inthemakingleadership.com/p/unlocked-the-30-day-boundary-setting

Hollister, K. (2025, June 30). *How to ask for space in a relationship: 5 Effective Ways*. Marriage Advice - Expert Marriage Tips & Advice. https://www.marriage.com/advice/relationship/how-to-ask-for-space-in-a-relationship/

Jenkins, M., & Jenkins, M. (2023, December 13). *Recovery from Narcissistic Abuse, Gaslighting, Codependency and Complex PTSD – By Linda Hill | Orange County Health Psychologists*. Orange County Health Psychologists | Integrated Care for Body, Mind and Spirit. https://www.ochealthpsych.com/recovery-from-narcissistic-abuse-gaslighting-codependency-and-complex-ptsd-by-linda-hill/

Kessler, O. (2025, February 20). *26 Examples of healthy boundaries in a relationship*. Marriage Advice - Expert Marriage Tips & Advice. https://www.marriage.com/advice/marriage-fitness/examples-of-healthy-boundaries-in-relationship/

Lcsw, F. W. (2025, May 20). *Why Women People-Please: Break free & find your true self — Francesca Wehr, LCSW*. Francesca Wehr, LCSW. https://francescawehrlcsw.com/pathways-to-wellness-insights-from-francesca-wehr-lcsw/people-pleasing-and-the-female-experience-unraveling-societal-expectations-and-embracing-authenticity

Lcsw, S. M. D. (2022, August 29). Boundaries can be good for you and those around you. *Psychology Today*. https://www.psychologytoday.com/us/blog/conquering-codependency/202208/6-ways-set-boundaries-without-guilt

Martin, S. (2025, May 27). *Managing Triggers When Setting Boundaries with Family*. Live Well With Sharon Martin. https://www.livewellwithsharonmartin.com/managing-triggers-when-setting-boundaries-with-family/

Maxfield, D., & Maxfield, D. (2025, December 24). *How to avoid social backlash in the workplace.* Crucial Learning. https://cruciallearning.com/blog/how-to-avoid-social-backlash-in-the-workplace/

McNamara, M. (2025, April 8). 12 Powerful Boundary-Setting Scripts to Say "No" Without Guilt. *Gentle Observations.* https://www.gentleobservations.com/post/12-powerful-boundary-setting-scripts-to-say-no-without-guilt?srsltid=AfmBOopA482H_Itc-4hRmJ9fKraAMLJqsZFrLtWJ6TYF0J-LS-3m1HX4

Medcalf, A., & Medcalf, A. (2024, August 6). *HOW TO IDENTIFY YOUR RELATIONSHIP BLIND SPOTS (PODCAST EPISODE 97).* Abby Medcalf. https://abbymedcalf.com/how-to-identify-your-relationship-blind-spots/

Nash, J., PhD. (2025, November 1). *How to set healthy boundaries & Build positive relationships.* PositivePsychology.com. https://positivepsychology.com/great-self-care-setting-healthy-boundaries/

Newman, J. (2025a, December 4). *How to set boundaries — examples and scripts* [Video]. Momentum Psychology. https://momentumpsychology.com/how-to-set-boundaries-examples-and-scripts/

Newman, J. (2025b, December 4). *How to set boundaries — examples and scripts* [Video]. Momentum Psychology. https://momentumpsychology.com/how-to-set-boundaries-examples-and-scripts/

Raypole, C. (2025, February 20). *30 Grounding techniques to quiet distressing thoughts*. Healthline. https://www.healthline.com/health/grounding-techniques

Rogers, A. (n.d.). *When to let go of a toxic relationship - Suicide Prevention Speakers | Mental Health Speakers*. Suicide Prevention Speakers | Mental Health Speakers. https://mentalhealthawarenesseducation.com/when-to-let-go-of-a-toxic-relationship/

Sutton, J., PhD. (2025a, June 13). *14 Worksheets for setting Healthy Boundaries*. PositivePsychology.com. https://positivepsychology.com/healthy-boundaries-worksheets/

Sutton, J., PhD. (2025b, June 13). *14 Worksheets for setting Healthy Boundaries*. PositivePsychology.com. https://positivepsychology.com/healthy-boundaries-worksheets/

Sutton, J., PhD. (2025c, June 30). *10 best Assertive communication Worksheets and Techniques*. PositivePsychology.com. https://positivepsychology.com/assertive-communication-worksheets/

Sutton, J., PhD. (2025d, June 30). *10 best Assertive communication Worksheets and Techniques*. PositivePsychology.com. https://positivepsychology.com/assertive-communication-worksheets/

The sensitivity of boundary setting in collectivist cultures. (n.d.). www.counseling.org. https://www.counseling.org/publications/counseling-today-magazine/article-archive/article/legacy/the-sensitivity-of-boundary-setting-in-collectivist-cultures

Therapy, E. Y. (2024, February 7). *How do you set boundaries with your In-Laws during the holidays?* Embracing You Therapy. https://embracingyoutherapy.com/set-boundaries-with-your-in-laws-during-the-holidays/

Villamor, M., & Villamor, M. (2023, December 30). *Navigating Boundaries: Strategies for Addressing Repeat Violations with Effective Consequences*. Terri Cole. https://www.terricole.com/boundary-violations/

Villamor, M., & Villamor, M. (2024, March 19). *Strategies + Scripts to start setting healthy boundaries with family*. Terri Cole. https://www.terricole.com/strategies-scripts-to-start-setting-boundaries-with-family/

Wellness, W. P. (2021, September 2). *10 tips to reduce Guilt about saying No*. Washington Psychological Wellness. https://washington-psychwellness.com/therapy/tips-to-reduce-guilt-about-saying-no/